MANAGING
BUBBIE

BY
RUSSEL LAZEGA

*For Bubbie, the yentas, and
the president, who never made it to brunch
with the family.*

The nine most terrifying words in the English language are,
"I'm from the government, and I'm here to help."
—Ronald Reagan

MANAGING BUBBIE
By: Russ Lazega

PROLOGUE
·······················

It was the last thing she said to me before I left for college. "I vant you should write these tings down," she told me. "Mine stories—mine life—I vant you should make a book from these tings, a book to tell vhat I did to bring mine children here to this country." I didn't pay her suggestion much mind at the time. Who had time for books?—What with entrance exams and fall fraternity rush coming up. Besides, I knew that in another week or so she'd be off on some other crusade—suing Ed McMahon or planning my wedding without even introducing me to the bride—there's always something. She's a page right out of a Neil Simon play, my grandmother, a true Miami Beach Jewish bubbie. Silver hair, tortoise-shell glasses two sizes too big, and that unmistakable Yiddish accent, "I vant you should make this book. You'll be my storyteller, my manager. You're a smart boy, Russel. A million dollars they'll pay you for this book! I know from these tings—I'm no dumb bubbie." I told her, somewhat insincerely, that I'd give it some thought. You've got to understand that once Bubbie has her mind set on something, there's no stopping her. "All my life I have miracles—A little angel on the shoulder that kept me alive from these tings I seen. Do you know from vat I'm saying—an angel?" Again, insincerely, I told her yes. But it wasn't for another ten years that I finally listened and understood what she meant—ten more years before I finally knew from angels.

A FAMILY AFFAIR

Summer 1987. Another holiday brunch at Mom's. My dad's cousin Leon is entrenched in another of his debates with my grandmother. He's not a bad guy, Leon—what you might call a character—he's loud, bald, and abrasively Russian. Right now he's playing a classical piece on an ebony piano with sticky keys. His gift for music was his father's legacy. The strained melody seems to smother an odd discussion that has turned...well, downright peculiar.

Leon:
Let me get this straight, Lea, you're telling me
Ronald Reagan is your long-lost half brother?

Bubbie:
Ya. I have a theory this vas the son from mine
father. Don't laugh. I have proof from these tings.

She reaches into her bag, fumbling through half-eaten Belgian chocolates and packets of Sweet and Low until finally, she pulls out an old photograph. It's black and white. Creases run down the middle. A date is scribbled on the back—1902.

Bubbie:
Look on this picture of mine father, and you tell me.

The resemblance to the archconservative is noteworthy, but hardly cause to call the six o'clock news.

Bubbie:
Just look on this face.

She places the photo beside a tabloid clipping of the president with his arm around the Close Encounters alien. The headline reads, "Reagan Consults with Extra-Terrestrial Ambassador."

1

Bubbie:

It must be. Look on the pictures. I tink this is my long-lost brother.

Leon:

What, ET or Reagan?

She remains steady in the face of a hostile brunch crowd.

Bubbie:

I have proof. Look, I vas born nineteen hunderd eleven. Reagan, he was born nineteen hunderd ten, almost the same time as me.

Leon:

Yeah, you and about a million other people.

Bubbie:

No listen, there's more. Mine father, he liked to chase women. He vas charming. How do you call it?—A card shark, a hustler. He used to make games and fighting matches in the park. He called it show business. Vell, anyvay, I tink he met this woman—this Mrs. Reagan—in one of these fights.

Leon:

Oh for crying out loud, Lea, your father barely spoke two words of English.

Bubbie:

This doesn't matter. He vas very handsome. Believe me, he'd find a vay.

Leon:

Right, it was a magical romance between a wealthy American woman and a piss-poor Polish Jew—

Never mind that he couldn't speak English and lived halfway around the world in Poland.

Bubbie:
No, no, no. Mine parents were here in America. They came here nineteen hunderd six.

Leon:
Your parents immigrated to America?

Bubbie:
Ya, they vent to California to look for gold.

Leon:
Gold? In 1906?

He's puzzled for a moment, and then, strangely, it makes sense.

Leon:
Sure, naturally, it probably took fifty years for the news to hit Poland.

Bubbie:
Mine parents came to America nineteen hunderd six, and then nineteen hunderd eleven they moved back to Poland. My mother vas pregnant mit me vhen they left here. So, mine sister vas born here a citizen, but I vas born in Poland.

Leon:
Sure, why stay in America—the land of opportunity—when you can live with the anti-Semites in Poland? Who wouldn't miss the lootings, the burnings, the Cossacks, the pogroms...

Bubbie:

Ach, vat can I tell you, when they finally got here
mine father didn't like it. He said it vas because
he didn't find any gold and because Jewish show
business vasn't good here. But I tink it vas because
he made this Irish girl pregnant, and they chased
him out from the city.

My green-haired teenage sister enters the room.

Leon:

Hey, Betsy, guess what, the president is your long-
lost great uncle.

Betsy:

Cool.

She's not impressed with her newfound political roots.

Leon:

Hey Lea, how's this? I say we take whole family on
trip to Washington to break the news to Reagan
that he's Jewish. His wife will love it. We'll bring
an orthodox rabbi with a black hat and a beard to
make a conversion. I'll even book "Sife the knife" to
do the circumcision.

Bubbie:

I know, I know, it sounds crazy, but vat can I tell
you? My life—oy!—my life is full of crazy stories.

CHAPTER I

HOMEWARD BOUND?

··

Her name is Lea, though in more trying times she's been Lila, Lodzia, and even a fugitive from the Reich. These days she's just Bubbie—Grandma. She was born in 1911, in Lodz, Poland, a run-down industrial town about a half -day west of Warsaw. She was the youngest of three children, whose parents had returned to Poland from the United States, where they had taken a failed stab at show-biz production. Isaac, Lea's father, had tried to organize and promote a Jewish theater company. One problem—there were no Jews in the rugged American West.

He had dragged his wife, his young son, and a scrappy little circus dog halfway around the world to find his fortune in California. Maybe fame, maybe gold—whatever was to be, America was where it all would happen. That's where he would find his dreams—in America.

But after five years of failure, he had bounced from town to town, odd job to odd job, only to end up penniless on a rickety freighter back to Poland. By that point, he and his wife, Esther, had their second child— a daughter named Evelyn—and another was coming. Soon.

Esther's delicate condition allowed her certain privileges on the ship. The crew cleared space for her alongside the cargo hold, where she and a few other women cared for their children. It was the only place in steerage that wasn't packed shoulder to shoulder with people.

You see, in 1911 there were a whole lot of people coming to America, but there were also a whole lot leaving. For every eight people who ventured to the land of opportunity, one would return to the squalor from whence he crawled, because maybe life was actually better there. If ships bound for America were ships of dreams, then the ships leaving were ships of broken dreams—rat-infested steel tubs brimming with desperate, shattered souls.

—⚏—

But Isaac Winter wasn't the sort to wallow. He kept busy on deck, entertaining onlookers with his violin, and he ran card games to round up a few bucks. His little dog, Zola, a spotted circus outcast, stayed at his ankle—always.

As for Esther, she couldn't sit still long in steerage, knowing that Isaac could be up to no good on deck. She gathered the children and went topside to put an end to whatever nonsense he was up to. He was leaning over a rail, staring intently at a woman on the deck below, when she found him.

That son of a bitch! He's at it again, she thought. Isaac was known to flirt. "If you spent half as much time looking for work as you do for wine and women, I swear I'd be the richest woman in all of Poland!"

Isaac tried to settle her. "No, no, look over there, down below, it's Millie Plotkin, the actress." At that time, Millie Plotkin was a pretty famous actress in European Jewish circles, which really wasn't such a big circle, but to someone striving to break into the business, she was big news.

"Come, Esther, let's go speak with her," Isaac begged, knowing damn well her usual answer.

"I have no interest in meeting theater actresses," Esther snapped.

Isaac tried again, for appearances' sake. "Please, Esther, darling, maybe she'll be interested in working with me."

"Working! What you do isn't working. It's hustling! Working men bring home money. They don't sit around the parks all day with filthy little animals."

As you've probably figured by now, Esther was a woman who wasn't afraid to speak her piece, or shout her piece, as the case may be. She was on a singular mission: to make Isaac a proper husband.

—⚏—

See, their marriage had been arranged by their parents, some say as a last measure of spite in a bitter family feud, but it was probably just bad judgment. Nonetheless, if she was stuck with a lemon, she was determined to make lemonade. Isaac would learn the stock of righteous Jewish men, like leading prayers at the dinner table and crying the ancient rites at the synagogue.

But after eight years of Esther shoving prayer books under his nose, the closest Isaac ever came to giving a religious invocation was shouting, "For G-d's sake, woman, would you let me drink in peace?" As for services, he tried going a couple times but was never quite welcome there after he swindled the rabbi out of his gold watch in a card game.

—m—

"You hear that, Isaac?" Esther bellowed. "The men are making a minion for that little boy who died from typhus. I want you to go with them to pray—and don't you dare bring any cards."

Isaac thought for a moment. "I'll tell you what, I'll make you a deal. I'll go to the service if you can survive two hours without nagging me."

"Fine." Esther was up to the challenge.

Needless to say, two hours later, while pious Jews were ensconced in prayer, Isaac and his dog were halfway to the bottom of a bottle of bourbon on deck. That's where he saw her again—you know, the not-so-famous, famous actress.

He blurted a snide comment, loud enough for her to hear, but directed away so as to appear as though somehow his remark wasn't meant for her. "I saw your play *The Witch* in San Francisco. I think it could have been much better."

She was captivated by the criticism. "Oh really, how's that?"

"It would've been better if you played the lead. Nadia Gould doesn't have nearly your beauty and depth of character. Besides, she's gotten so fat, the set shakes when she makes her entrance. Of course, that's not to say that casting Nadia as the star of a play called *The Witch* was an altogether bad idea."

The actress chuckled. She stared at Isaac for a moment and then at her cigarette. She tried to appear more interested in the cigarette than in Isaac. "Are you always so full of shit?"

"Was I really that transparent?" he whispered.

"Like glass." She took a drag of her cigarette. "So, do you really think I'd have been better than Nadia?"

Isaac slid closer and stole a drag. "I think you'd have been amazing."

It was right then that he heard it, a shrill cry in the distance drawing nearer—"Isaac Winter, I curse you! May you be turned on your head, buried deep in the ground, and then sprout back up like an onion!"

Esther had a gift for finding a party—and stamping it out. As usual, her timing was impeccable.

So it ended. Isaac slithered back to his family without another word. He had given up long ago trying to explain his indiscretions. The actress disappeared into the crowd—forever.

IMPARTING IS SUCH SWEET SORROW

Family brunch can be an exercise in comparative misery. Distant relatives twelve times removed travel from far up the street to relive old wrongs and resurrect fights long forgotten. They stop for fish and a few short words, quibble over quiz shows and return to their worlds full from the day and the morning's quarrels. I guess it's a brief break from the South's summer heat, which blisters and boils, festering new waves of old complaints.

Bubbie:

Oy, this heat!

It always starts like that. Eyes half-closed, head tilted to the sky, she fans herself with last Sunday's TV Guide.

Bubbie:

I should have stayed in Poland. Maybe they tried to
kill us all the time, but at least over there you could
go outside vit-out fainting.

Not to be outdone, Leon shouts above a tenderly played Tchaikovsky.

Leon:

Why the hell did your parents go back to Poland?
I don't know why any Jew in his right mind would
ever go to Poland. They're the biggest anti-Semites
in the world—the Poles—worse than the Germans,
worse than the Russians. At least the Russians
treated us all the same—they shipped us all to
Siberia. Da, it's nothing but ice and bugs the size of
your head—Siberia. You think this is miserable—
spend week in gulag with no boots or coat.

Bubbie:

Ach, Poland vas no picnic either. I remember vhen I vas a little girl, the president from Poland got a Jewish mistress. Vell, this mistress vanted to make things better for the Jewish people. So she asked her boyfriend, this president, to put the Polish children together mit the Jewish children in school. Anyvay, vhat's he gonna say—this mashugina president? He listened to the mistress and made a law that all the Jewish children had to leave the Jewish schools and go to Polish schools. Bap! Just like that—the next day we vere all in Polish schools mit the Polish children, and they gave me a Polish name—"Lodzia." Ach, Leon, these Polish kids vere so mean. They spit on us, they hit us, they tooked our shoes and coats and pushed us into the snow.

Leon:

Da, it's all Reagan's fault.

Bubbie:

Vhat do you get that it's Reagan's fault? Ach, that's another story—Reagan. Anyvay, I promise mineself then that I'm going to go to America—No matter vat, I'm going to follow my sister to the greatest country in the world—America.

I just don't get it. They're actually arguing over whose life was more miserable? Maybe there's a certain satisfaction in sharing your troubles and, I suppose, sheer ecstasy in knowing that they're even worse than the next guy's.

For me, I just try to tune it out and turn on the TV. The couch is cozy and $25,000 Pyramid is buzzing in anxious anticipation of the Smolensky Sisters—loud, pumpkin-shaped Brooklyn wom-en, who must be seen to be explained.

So, for now, I wait. I've been\through enough of these to know that it's all just beginning, and by the start of the Dating Game, it'll all be over, and each of us, if we listen close, will leave a little fuller. See, my perspective is just a little distinct from theirs. I know no atrocities. I live in a warm, sunny place where time is measured by the television set, and life could never be any differ-ent than the world I'm just beginning to know.

CHAPTER II

POLAND

·····················

It wasn't long before the family had settled back in Lodz, a Polish town known for, well, known for nothing. Money was tight. What little they'd had Isaac squandered on his play for stardom in America. They took a small two-room apartment near the German market. To make ends meet, Isaac sold show tickets at the jewish theater. During intermissions, he hustled cards. In traditional Jewish fashion, Esther stayed home to care for the children. By this point, she had given birth to their third child. They named her Lea, in memory of Isaac's mother.

Jews have this tradition of naming their children after a loved one who has recently passed. It's a way of forging an eternal bond between generations—a sort of circle of immortality. A radiant young child will forever wear a legacy bequeathed by a relative she will never know. It's a small semantic link that binds the child to her past and carries her past into the future—each whisper of her name breathes life into a dying memory.

As far as Esther was concerned, it was just a crafty way for Isaac to resurrect an obstinate old goat that she finally had the good fortune to bury. Her mother-in-law was finally gone, and Esther wasn't about to bring her back—not for tradition or anyone else's sake. She ranted and raved, hollered and screamed, but Isaac was settled. Just this once, he would get his way—his daughter would be called Lea.

This Lea inherited much from her namesake—a plump, round face, headstrong ways, and paper-thin patience. The fact was, nobody was ready for a baby—not then, not yet. The economy was in the dumps. The world was bracing for war. And crowded lives had just become a lot more crowded.

But naturally, Esther had a plan. She knew that by bringing in boarders to share the rent, they could afford a bigger place. Of course, she also figured that for the right price she could fill every bed in the house—and then some. By the time Isaac and the others were ready to move into their spacious six-room apartment, Esther had rented five rooms to four families.

—⁓—

If life was uncomfortable in two rooms, then it was unbearable in one. There were actors, musicians, prop makers, a goose dealer...

But to her credit, the boarders did bring in money—nearly enough to cover the rent. Of course, as quickly as Esther could earn it, Isaac would piddle it away on some foolishness. He bought fine clothes, backed failed production after failed production, and hired the best music teacher in town to teach his boy, Abraham, the violin.

At nights, Isaac would show off his gifted son to the other housemates. "A star, I tell you. One day this little one will be more famous than Strauss," he'd boast. "Listen to him play. I could never play like that when I was twelve."

"You can't play like that now," the boarders would joke.

They were right. Isaac had passion, but Abraham had talent. Crowds would gather to listen to the young prodigy and his singing violin—everyone but Esther, that is. She didn't understand this obsession with music, with stardom and attention. "The violin is a toy," she'd say. "You should teach him a trade—something handy." Esther's opinion aside, Isaac kept encouraging his son not to be handy. He'd take Abe to recitals, to parks, to pubs—anywhere that someone might hear him play.

Eventually someone did. Abe earned an invitation to one of Poland's finest music academies.

With star-glazed eyes, Isaac and Abraham raced home to tell Esther the good news. "Esther, Esther, my love," Isaac cried, "you won't believe it. The Warsaw Youth Conservatory has accepted our boy! Abe is going to study with the greatest musicians in all of Poland."

Esther was not impressed. "You want to spend good money to send a twelve-year-old child all the way to Warsaw for what? So he can play with toys? For this you could send him to a kindergarten. No, I will not allow it. My son will learn to make a living."

Abe was furious. "I hate you," he blasted her. "You are not my mother! From now on, I have no mother." And from that day forward, he didn't. He stayed under her roof, but counted the days until he could leave and never look back.

The conservatory had been Abe's dream, and now that his mother had forbidden him to go, it was his mission. For months, he snuck out his window in the middle of the night—violin in hand—and played in the market streets for change. It took nearly a year, but eventually, he panhandled enough to attend the music institute. Quietly, packing little more than his violin, he hopped a train and left with no good-byes.

As always, Esther wasn't far behind. She followed on the next train to Warsaw and dragged her son back to Lodz, away from the sort of trouble that makes people famous. No child of hers would piddle away his days playing Mozart. To set him right, she sent him to work for Herschel, the bald-headed barber. Maybe there he could learn something useful. Abe quietly raged at the injustice, vowing beneath his breath that when he grew up he would never let his children do anything useful.

—⁂—

By the summer of 1920, life in Lodz was changing. Still, the boom of progress and prosperity seemed to be rippling past Poland. Lodz was like a dingy hovel with a wide-open view of a vibrant, bustling new world. Everything—movies, automobiles, telephones—all of it was close enough to see, hear, and smell, but never reach. On the radio, German program announcers tirelessly hawked "the liberating experience" of the automobile, "the convenience" of refrigerators and toasters, and a thousand other things working Jews could never afford. Meanwhile, French and American magazines showered the country with glossy images of glamorous models driving glamorous cars to glamorous mansions—no doubt stocked to the ceiling with refrigerators and toasters. The new generation was fast realizing that it was no longer enough to walk in their parents' shoes. Yep, maybe life was changing, but Poland wasn't.

—〰—

As for Abe, he was fifteen, ambitious, and ready to take on the world. With hardly a thought, he took what money he had, borrowed a little more, and bought himself a shiny black motorcycle—the only one in the neighborhood. After all, he was a local celebrity and had an image to maintain. Folks in town were raving about the brave young barber who had saved a little girl from drowning in a cesspool. See, like I said, Poland was still a hundred or so years behind the times, so most people didn't have electricity or indoor plumbing. There were outhouses. Well, a local girl, a skinny little rag child, had fallen through the toilet into the cesspool below. Abe was working outside when he heard her scream.

Instinctively, he kicked open the door, ripped out the seat, and fished the little girl from the foul sludge. They were both covered in shit. No other way to say it—they were covered with shit. Abe became a hero for diving into the shit, and the little girl became a laughingstock for falling in it. It got so bad the child's family eventually packed up and moved to Palestine—they couldn't very well have their daughter growing up being called the "Shit Girl" for the rest of her life. As luck would have it, by fleeing to the desert, that Shit Girl's family escaped the horrors that followed during the war in Europe—all because their daughter fell through the john. Funny how fate works that way.

That's how things were in Poland, simple but complicated—the steady madness of a world that was never quite right. Evelyn couldn't run from it fast enough. By thirteen she was already planning her return to America. Poland had nothing for her. She wanted to see cities and lights and people—just like in the magazines. These Jews in Poland were like rabbis—drowned in scripture, buried in books. They were old and crusty and spoke in riddles—questions were answers, answers were questions—their lives interminably pinned to the study of learning more. But for all they read, they never explored, they never touched, they never embraced life. Evelyn was ambitious and even early on knew she wanted more than a backward Polish town could ever offer. She'd stay up at night telling Lea how one day she'd live in America—a land of opportunity and cinema houses—a land where children didn't fall into their own filth.

—◊—

None of it made any sense to Lea yet. Valentino or not, life beyond Lodz hardly seemed worth the trouble. "There are worse places than Poland." That's how she saw it, so she stuck to home, with its old ways and fashions. I guess at heart she was all frills and bows, though a part of her quietly envied Evelyn's unabashed willingness to bob her hair and wear trousers in public.

So the years crept by, and life dragged on. And for a brief while, things weren't too bad, even by Jewish standards. Isaac began to make a name for himself at the theater and even managed to save enough to move the family to an apartment almost their own.

Things finally seemed to be turning around for Isaac, and he was looking like a new man. His suits were fine and fitted. His hair, black and full from a fresh summer shave. A hundred zloties* and a promise of discretion about temple finances had even bought him the seat of honor at the synagogue—right beside the pulpit. The game, it seems, was on again.

But reality was, he spent what he had—and then borrowed what he didn't have. And by now, the well was bone-dry. Still, something

---

* Polish dollars

told him he was climbing to greater things—more than shuffling shells on the sanctuary steps. He was finally inside—in the spotlight—where fortunes were made.

So he set up shop within the shul,* waiting for his mark. After all, no good gossip could possibly let pass the story of how Isaac Winter managed to tumble ass over teakettle into that kind of money. And naturally, Isaac did what any keen salesman would do: he lied. "What, you haven't been to my new show? It's quite the hit. I'm shocked you haven't seen it." Well, one thing led to another, and before you knew it, folks were packing the theater and dumping in money. The truth is, it was a good performance—he just needed to make them believe it.

But as fast as fortune came, it fled. Straight jobs just didn't agree with Isaac, and by the start of the New Year's service, he had managed to lose it all in a shell game to the town's new swindler. And while Isaac was never the sort to cry, that day the tears rained like the great flood of old. So much so that it stopped the service. But, as always, Isaac kept his cool. He straightened his coat, cleared his throat, and with the wit of an old fox answered the crowd, "My friends, I weep for the destruction of the ancient temple." And the congregation agreed...there could be no greater loss.

But something was lost that New Year's morning, and Isaac was never the same. Tensions in the house soared, and gradually, the family parted. Abe married Malcha, a little dancer from down the hall and moved in next door to his in-laws. Evelyn eventually found her way home to America. And Isaac was finally able to avoid Esther's watchful eye for long enough to meet another woman. Just before Lea's twelfth birthday, he ran off with her, leaving nothing but a mountain of debt.

Lea and Esther were alone and broke. But if that husband had taught her anything, it was that where there's a wit, there's a way.

And so, later the next day a deal was done. Esther sold their home for 130 American dollars to two fat American missionaries who had come to help the Polish children. No notice, no warning, Lea just came

* Synagogue

home from school one day, and they were homeless. They watched the young missionaries move furniture into their home—such beautiful furnishings, rich wood, velvet pillows, puffy cushions. Lea and Esther slept in the stairwell that night. It was so cold, so dark.

Poland was always an awful place to live, especially if you were homeless. Its dark streets reeked of nearby cesspools. The stench was especially foul when it rained, which seemed to be always that fall. It was a cold and constant rain that poured straight down like water from a bath faucet. Sometimes, when the storms came, the water flew sideways like tiny bullets launched by the howling wind. That night was a sideways rainy night, so the stairwell offered little shelter from the chilly sting of the flying teardrops.

Rain-soaked hat in hand, Esther foraged for work and finally took the only job she could—as the cook and maid in a whorehouse. At nights, if it was quiet and the madam said yes, Lea would hem dresses and fit corsets in the kitchen. When the girls were at work, she hid in the alley, behind the trash, like a homeless cat waiting at the porch step for dinner scraps. It was the only way at the time, but the madam was right. "A whorehouse is no place to raise a child." A baby should be with a family. The madam suggested a jeweler named Yenkel—an upright and righteous man who paid every bill, including hers, like clockwork. Yenkel often complained that his wife wasn't fit to care for a poodle, let alone two children. Esther knew right away it was perfect for Lea. Just imagine, a job like that would cover room and board and maybe even a little extra to help Mama.

The next morning, Esther marched down to Lea's school and withdrew her. Lea was only twelve at the time, eighteen months shy of the fourteen-year minimum dropout age, but that was nothing a few changes to a birth certificate couldn't fix. That afternoon, Lea, a baby herself, was a nanny.

But give her credit; though she was young and inexperienced, she had a natural hand with the children. She learned to feed them, clean them, entertain them, and do all those other things a twelve-year-old mother is supposed to do. Those girls were her world, but she never stopped longing for home. And though she resented her mother for abandoning her, there was still a part of her that missed the feeling of family—that security of knowing that, no matter what, your kin will always be there to provide unconditional torment. "Your mother is your mother, no matter what," she'd say. A studio, a warehouse, an alley— anywhere. Home is where your people are.

A few years later she got her chance. Isaac was back—broke and ready to start again. But change is a fickle friend. Esther and Isaac began bickering, which used to be a good sign that life was normal. But now things were different. It was an explosion of bitterness and resentment that had coiled and wound over decades. Isaac soon remembered why he left, and Esther remembered why she was glad that he had. In no time, it was over, and Isaac was gone again—this time forever.

MATCHMAKER, MATCHMAKER, LEAVE ME ALONE

My grandmother and Leon have tired of arguing for the moment, so I finally have a turn to talk with her—which, of course means another discussion about...

Bubbie:
> Russel, listen, I have a nice Jewish girl I vant you should meet.

Yup, here we go again.

Bubbie:
> She's just right for you. She's not too tall, and she's Jewish.

For those of you who are unfamiliar with the Jewish Grandmother National Dating Connection, let me take a moment to explain. Using the most sophisticated technology, Jewish grandmothers around the world are linked to an elaborate computer network specifically designed to find a perfect match for their grandsons. Of course, there are only two criteria to match: 1) not too tall and 2) Jewish. A guy could bring home a petite bank robber to meet his grandmother, and if she's Jewish, you can bet the farm that his bubbie will be telling the whole canasta club about what a nice Jewish girl her grandson met.

Me:
> Okay, Bubbie, what's her story?

Bubbie:
> She's a nice Jewish girl. Not too tall.

I'm going to need a little more to go on than that.

Me:

Uh huh...and where did you find her?

Bubbie:

I vas talking mit a neighbor from mine building—a Mrs. Finkelstein—and this Mrs. Finkelstein has a sister in Alaska mit a granddaughter your age in—

Me:

Bubbie, I'm not going to Alaska to meet some girl.

Bubbie:

Who says anyting about going to Alaska? Just listen. This Mrs. Finkelstein's sister's granddaughter goes away to college, and she's a nice Jewish girl.

Me:

And where does she live now?

Bubbie:

Close.

Me:

What's close? Ft. Lauderdale? Palm Beach?

Bubbie:

Philadelphia.

Me:

For crying out loud, Bubbie, that's two thousand miles away.

Bubbie:

She'll move to marry you. Don't you vorry, I'll take care on that.

Me:

That's what I'm afraid of.

Bubbie:

You just leave it to your bubbie.

That's how these things go with my grandmother. She's a firm believer that choosing one's eternal soul mate is a job best left to professionals. It's a philosophy that's been handed down by generations of very wise Jews who have figured, "Who knows better what the rest of us need than a mama or a bubbie?"

CHAPTER III

BESHERT

....

It was just Esther and Lea again, and that suited Esther just fine. Men were unreliable and generally more trouble than they were worth. Of course, those feelings aside, Esther continued to hunt tirelessly for her daughter's perfect match—her *beshert*—her "meant to be."

"Oh, if only Mendel the undertaker or Shalom the Shabbos klapper* would look my daughter's way," she'd beg the heavens. But Lea had other plans. She was a pretty girl—plump, not fat—with thick dark hair and gypsy eyes. She had just turned sixteen and was ready to conquer the world. A friend knew a friend who knew people in Brussels who could find her work in a textile mill. The pay was terrible, the job conditions worse, and the prospects for advancement nonexistent. The offer was irresistible.

That sunny Thursday morning she emptied her change from a sugar jar and set off for Belgium. Just like that, she was gone.

There was no plan, no papers, no direction but south.

---

* Guy hired by the synagogue to knock on people's window shutters with a hammer to alert them to the start of the Sabbath service.

May 19, 1927

My dearest Evelyn:

I did it! I finally did it! I took what I had and just left. The train got me to Germany, but then I had to stop, because the people said the Belgians wouldn't let you in without papers. I was the only one with no papers, so a man said to me, "Don't worry, leave the train, and walk that way to Belgium." Just like that. I didn't know where I was going, but I walked. It took me two days to cross the frontier through the wilderness. Oy, Evelyn, you couldn't imagine the creatures in those woods. Germany is a place of wolves. They were everywhere, howling all night long. And there was nothing there in that wilderness but me and them. Once in a while I'd find some trash on the ground—cigarette boxes, a piece of newspaper—things like that. It's how I knew where I was going. When the cigarette boxes started to be in French instead of German I knew I must be getting close. I just kept walking like that. Can you believe it? Me doing this myself. And now I'm here! Oh, Evelyn, Belgium is everything I dreamed about. It's like your magazine pictures. Don't worry, I'll be coming to you in America soon. But for now, I think I want to stay here.

All my love,

Lea

Brussels captured Lea from the moment she arrived. The city was young and alive. Lovers kissed at the foot of the town square fountain. Merchants bickered over the price of junk. Musicians played in the plaza for change. Lea was home.

But bliss was fast replaced by the burdens of a badly planned move. The train fare had cost forty-six zloties. Her savings totaled eighty. The remainder might last a week in such a fancy place. But at least for the moment, she was finally here—strolling and wandering, soaking in the aura of a real city. A plan? Well, that could wait…for now.

Broad cobblestone boulevards, lined with shiny cars and soft-lit chestnut trees, stretched in all directions. Endless glass storefronts—tall and bright—filled the walkways where pushcarts and shanties should have been. "So many things!" a girl in wonder marveled, shrieking and twirling at every indulgence she passed. The Boulevard du Midi gushed with riches even a princess couldn't imagine—treasure chests of jewels, dresses of silk—even a place filled with nothing but...chocolates! Belgium was a dream.

But dreams can be hollow without help to make them happen. So she set out searching for some familiar sliver of the world she knew. She set out for synagogue.

I guess it was fortunate that the rabbi's daughter was *meiskeit*,* which—forget what Hemingway said—is truly the worst form of unlucky. She was seventeen and single, and if something didn't happen soon she'd become an *alte moid*—an old maid—and then even the beggars would have to lend pity.

"I think she just needs someone to talk with her," the rabbi fretted. So many suitors had fled in thunderstorms of fits and tears. "Maybe a girl closer to her own age might help her understand. Maybe a friend might help her settle on a husband." And so he said, "Lea, please stay."

What could she say? It was a home. But there was just something about that question that the rabbi first asked her—"Don't you have anyone here, darling?"—that rang in her head and reminded her that she had to keep moving, to find her own home, to build her own family.

—⟋⟍—

Back in the day, in a time when she could still clearly remember her father's face, he had given her something. It's funny. She had never thought much of it until now. Most of what he'd left her was usually fast followed by a "rightful owner" wanting it back. But this one she had saved. It was just a note—rolled and squeezed into her hand with a

---

* A person with a face only a mother could love.

gentle instruction. "If you ever need help…go to her." Scribbled on the back of an old Yiddish show flyer was the name "Faygala Goldblum" and the address "14 Rue de Jardins, Brussels, Belgium." She was Isaac's sister. She'd left Poland some time ago back when things were just bad. He said she'd married a truckload of money and somehow landed here.

Of course, Lea wouldn't dare show up, suitcase in hand, at the door-step of a relative she'd never even met. So she decided instead to write her aunt a letter explaining who she was and that she wanted to see her.

Naturally, Faygala was suspicious. Stories of this sort of thing were rampant—crafty foreigners who would show up pitiful and ragged at your door, pretending to be distant family, and then make off with your silver. But curiosity compels, and so Faygala agreed to meet outside a curbside cafe.

That morning Lea wore her nicest dress—white with pink flowers and a little white bow at the neckline. Her dark bobbed hair was pinned back on one side with a bow just like the one on her dress. On her feet, simple white shoes with little white bows.

Aunt Faygala wasn't hard to spot. Traditionally, religious Jewish women are distinctly modest. They wear long dark dresses and cover their heads with scarves, hats, or wigs. As far as fashion goes, wealthy re-ligious Jewish women have it a little better. They wear long, dark, tailored dresses, accessorized with fur stoles, elegant hats, and exquisite jewelry.

Lea timidly approached the glittering little woman in the pillbox hat. "Tanta Faygala? Aunt Faygala?" she asked, uncertain whether to call this tiny stranger her aunt.

"Come closer, child, let me get a look at you," the woman mumbled. She called Lea child, though they stood eye to eye.

"What did you say your name was, child?"

"Lea…Lea Winter," she stumbled.

Faygala studied her closely, circling a few times to get a view from all sides.

"Lea Winter? That was my mother's name," Faygala said as she stopped mid-turn to rummage through her bag. She fished out a faded photo of a silver-haired woman and handed it to Lea. "My mother—Lea Winter. You look just like her—it's in the eyes. I knew it when I saw you."

Lea didn't see the resemblance to the shriveled old woman in the picture, but wasn't about to argue her way out of a home.

"This was my grandmother?" Lea asked.

"Yes, child, your Bubbie Lea. Now grab your things and come on home with me." There were no hugs, no tears, no kisses—that was just Faygala's way. She walked to the driver's side window of the car and rapped her diamond ring on the glass to wake the snoozing driver. "Come, Simcha, it's time to go." She waved a silk-gloved hand for Lea to grab her things and follow. The man in the car stumbled out from behind the wheel to help with the bags. He was fat, sweaty, with a long ash-gray beard, a brown fur hat and a heavy wool coat. "Lea, this is your uncle Simcha," Faygala muttered. He smiled at her warmly and nodded. Again, there were no hugs, no tears, no kisses. That was their way.

Fourteen Rue des Jardins was like nothing she had ever seen—well, except maybe in her sister's magazines. It covered nearly half the block and was three stories tall. The brass chandelier, the hand-carved furniture, the gray stone facade, everything there was so old. Lea ran her fingers across a mahogany foyer table. Such old furniture looked like it should be dusty, but everything was spotless. Perched atop the dark-grained table was a clay vase with a chipped handle. It looked ancient enough to be something Moses had drunk from. Lea stared at the vase for a bit, wondering why anyone would flaunt broken kitchenware.

—ɱ—

In the kitchen, things were bustling in preparation for dinner—pots clanked, silver clinked, a bell dinged. And then things got quiet. Faygala and her four children hurried across the house and gathered in the kitchen where they joined Simcha, who was already waiting to lead the family in prayers and ritual hand washing. The room was pin-drop silent as Simcha grabbed an overfilled silver pitcher and splashed the water three times over each hand. He set the jug on the counter, muttered a short prayer, and motioned Lea to follow. She tried to imitate her uncle, but the pitcher was too heavy, and she spilled water all over her new shoes. Lea chuckled at her clumsiness. The rest of the crowd just stared with quiet disapproval. Faygala signaled a servant to clean the mess and then took her place at the table.

More prayers. Simcha blessed everything in sight, and then things got quiet again for a bit. Everyone seemed to be waiting for someone else to make a first move. They just chewed and stared at each other, patiently fishing for something meaningful to say. Finally, Simcha broke the ice.

"So, Lea, what do you plan to do for work?" Simcha asked—his mouth half-full of hen.

"I have a job sewing in a factory," she answered. The family looked at each other as though someone had something to say that wasn't being said. "Don't worry," Lea quickly added, "I'll have money to pay you a little for rent. I know it's not nearly enough for—"

"Oh, no, no," Simcha interrupted, "I don't want your money. You're family. I just figured if you needed work, we could find something for you at my factory. I sell shoemaker's supplies."

Lea didn't want to impose any more than she already had. Besides, she had moved to Belgium to find her own path. "Oh, thank you, Uncle, but I really like my job. I know I don't make that much, but I really should pay you something."

"You let us worry about the rent, child," Faygala interjected. "You just save your money for a rainy day when you need it."

—◊—

So, each week, the same conversation would be repeated. Lea would offer Faygala half of her wages. Faygala would humbly refuse. They'd quibble a bit—you know—a you-take-the-money-no-you-keep-the-money sort of argument, and then Aunt Faygala would finally accept the rent under protest. "If you insist. Such a responsible girl, you are," she'd say.

But soon, the stagnation became too much, and it was finally time for Lea to find a place of her own. Faygala and Simcha were the picture of kindness, but she would never feel like their home was hers. She would always be the round peg squeezing into the square hole.

One morning during breakfast, she broke the news to Faygala. "Tanta Faygala, I'm moving." She didn't know any other way to say it but to blurt it all out. Lea was surprised by how unsurprised Faygala was.

"I knew you wouldn't stay," Faygala said as she marched into the kitchen, trailed by a speechless Lea. "You're a traveler, like my mother. You need to always be moving around and going places. This life isn't for you." Faygala smiled at Lea for a moment and then grabbed a nearby chair, which she climbed to reach the top cupboard. There, stashed behind some old pots and pans, was a jar full of money. It was the rent that Lea had been paying her—every penny of it—saved for that rainy day. "For your travels," Faygala said as she handed the jar to Lea.

The next morning, Lea woke early to begin her move. She tried to leave without a tumult—without a commotion—but everyone was waiting at the door to wish her well. Again, there were no hugs, no tears, no kisses—just a few smiles. It was their way. Lea cried and hugged her family. Their way wasn't hers.

A NOSE FOR TROUBLE

I've never been much of a Jew. Truth is, being Jewish has often been a whole lot of trouble.

"Forget about football practice—you've got Haftorah lessons."

"You can't eat pizza—it's Passover."

"Your brother needs a nose job before you."

And then there's that Jewish calendar where every holiday miraculously falls on the same day as the greatest sporting events of the season. I think the problem is we Jews just don't march to the same drum as the rest of the world.

So nowadays, I show up at synagogue for the occasional high holiday, wash down crisp bacon with a cool glass of milk, and after fourteen years of the finest Hebrew instruction on the planet, I've managed to learn how to say "Ani rotze lelechet l'beyt shmoosh"—"I need to go to the shitter."

Yep, we Lazegas have a long and not-so-proud history of hovering tenuously on the fringe of Jewish society.

It's true. For generations, while pious and virtuous men bobbed and weaved in trancelike prayer reaching for new heights of mysticism and spiritual understanding, we swindled their tzedakah* money and rallied revolutions. But they never turned us away—not ever.

Bubbie says that during the war, being Jewish made her a target, but it also kept her alive—a blessed curse woven deep into her soul. Maybe that's why she's got this unbending commitment to a faith she hardly practices. It's also the reason there are subjects around which this family treads lightly.

---

* Charity

See, for what feels like ages, I've been hiding a secret. I dodge and duck the issue every way I can, but I know at some point it's got to come out. Somehow, though, some other time always seems better. So, for now I stay silent—killing time on the couch, praying she doesn't go there—just me, Bubbie, and Dick Clark over there squawking on a Sony big screen.

Bubbie, though, has her eye on a different show. She's studying me quietly, as she always does when she's up to trouble. It's like she smells that something's amiss and swoops right in to shatter the ice.

Bubbie:

You know vhy you're losing your hair?

Ouch! That one I wasn't expecting.

Me:

Why's that, Bubbie?

Bubbie:

It's because you don't have a nice Jewish girl to take care on you.

I'd thought that—like most of my problems—"heredity" was the answer.

Me:

Bubbie, there's plenty of time for that.

Bubbie:

Alvays with you it's "there's time." There's no time for me! I'm not getting any younger, you know, and I vant more than anyting I should live to dance on your vedding. Don't you vorry, I'm gonna find a nice Jewish girl for you.

Just know, when she says "don't worry"—I worry.

_Me:_

Bubbie, I'm okay, really. I've got a lot of things
going on and—

Bubbie:

Never mind, I'll take care on it.

Man, I want to tell her—to just spit it out and shout that I've met
a girl and it's serious. I want to scream that she's cute and clever and headstrong and...Cuban...Catholic, with...gasp...a cross
around her neck.

So my mind races from reason to random as I wonder about
what she'll do when she sees that crucifix. It's gold and shiny,
and for both Jews and vampires crosses are like Raid. So, I imagine a scene like Bela Lugosi in those old Dracula movies—that
she'll hiss, throw her arm over her eyes, and run out of the room
screaming that we haven't seen the last of her.

Quickly, I try to take her somewhere else—far from
Transylvania and our petty secrets.

_Me:_

Bubbie, you know I'm working on that book about
your stories.

Bubbie:

Good. Good. Write down these tings vhat I tell you.
People need to hear vhat ve vent through, vhat ve
suffered to be Jewish. Ach, today, the young people
don't care anymore about the Jewish vays. They
don't understand. Look at your cousin. Can you
believe it? He married an Irish girl.

There went my case for established precedent.

Bubbie:

Okay, at least I don't vorry about you. I know you vouldn't do that to us.

She says "us" as though the fate of all Judaism rested squarely in my cream-cheese-covered hands. Funny thing is, in her own mixed-up way, she's kind of right. The truth is, we lose more Jews to attrition and indifference than Hitler could ever have taken. Think about it—in a world of billions—the people who fathered the faiths of half the planet number about thirteen million. We're barely a blip on the radar, and nobody's worrying but the bubbies.

Bubbie:

Okay, at least you're not like that other cousin. You understand these tings—vhat it is to be Jewish.
All right, vhat can ve do? I love her too now—she's family. At least she got a Jewish nose. I tink maybe once upon a time her relatives must have been from our people. The Catholics don't got these noses. All right, all right, let it be...She's a nice girl...Maybe she'll convert.

Every bit of reason in my body tells me I shouldn't have to explain who I fell in love with, but there I go slithering into the closet right beside gay cousin Stanley and Avi Frankel's daughter who ran off with her Lacrosse coach.

Me:

Yeah, Bubbie—not me. I get it.

CHAPTER IV
A MATCH MADE IN POLAND

···

It didn't take Lea long to find a place of her own. It wasn't much—a ratty studio apartment in the commercial quarter of Brussels—but it was home, and it was hers. She was independent and earning her own keep, and she even managed to put aside a bit for Mama.

Naturally, Esther felt it wiser to spend the money on train fare to Belgium than lining some fat landlord's pockets. After all, Poland hadn't produced a suitable husband for her daughter; maybe Belgium would be better. "A wealthy Polish Jew, a wealthy Belgian Jew," she figured. "What difference does it make, so long as he's wealthy and Jewish?" So, undaunted by her failures at home, Esther packed her things and headed to Belgium.

Despite being new to the country and not speaking a lick of French, Esther was remarkably adept at finding prospective suitors. After only the briefest procession of gravediggers and toothless widowers—success!

"Lea, my sweet Lea! I have wonderful news. I have found your perfect husband!" Esther could barely contain her excitement, quite uncharacteristic of the woman who was rumored to only once before have broken a smile. "Lea, you must come see him!"

Lea was not anxious to marry. "Please, Mama, I'm not ready to get married yet."

"I won't hear it," Esther barked. "I've found you a good man who makes a nice living."

Lea was not convinced. "He's probably fat and bald, with a face like a prune. I won't marry him!"

Esther had tried reason to no avail. Now it was time for guilt. She gripped her chest, one hand atop the other, as if to support a heart sinking with grief. Her breath grew shallow and strained, "Oy, the pain—such pain. I work for years all night long, cooking and cleaning, stitching and pinning, so that I can give you food and a home—by myself I do this, no husband—and this is how you repay me? I give you a chance to make a good life with a nice man—a rich nice man—and you make jokes. Oy, the Lord should take me now, quickly, so I shouldn't suffer anymore."

Lea began to cave. "Okay, Mama, who is he?"

Esther's flight from the grip of death was swift. "Jacob, Jacob the tailor from your factory," she stammered excitedly. "I must go and tell him the news! Did I mention that he makes a nice living?"

It was all that Esther could dream for her daughter—to be the wife of a tradesman. But Lea was unsettled about her sudden engagement. She was only seventeen and hadn't even begun to think of marriage, especially to an old fossil who was already well into his twenties. The day after Esther raced off to accept Jacob's proposal, Lea ran away to the docks of Antwerp.

Her plan was simple. Find a freighter heading to America, get a job as a cabin girl, and jump ship once the boat reached the United States. There she'd be safe with her sister—far away from mothers and wrinkled husbands.

So, she made her way to the port of Antwerp and the one ship that was Brooklyn-bound. Crusty sailors were loading cargo from the pier. Bashfully, she approached a young crewman and asked for the captain. A bald sailor with a curled mustache lowered his crates and spoke for the captain.

"He's busy, what do you want?"

"I'm-I'm looking for work as a cleaning girl on the ship," she stuttered.

The smooth-headed man studied her for a moment and asked her age. At first Lea thought to say twenty-two, but she knew she'd never pass for older than nineteen, so that's what she said. Besides, her birth certificate backed up her story—Mama had seen to that.

The crewman unfurled his mustache and deliberated for a moment. His hollow eyes rolled up and down as he considered the situation. "Nineteen, you say? I'd have figured you for sixteen, maybe seventeen. Well, it doesn't matter anyway, because I can't let you work on the ship until you're twenty-one. Why don't you come back in a couple years."

Lea begged and pleaded, but there was no changing his mind. "Captain's rules."

She hadn't thought of a backup plan. She had just figured on boarding the boat to America. Aside from cleaning ships, there wasn't much use for young girls in Antwerp. So, defeated and despondent, Lea returned to Brussels to accept her prune-faced destiny.

And so it was. Without courtship or romance, the couple was married a month later in a simple Jewish ceremony. All in all, it really wasn't a bad match. Sure, maybe he was short and skinny like a piece of string, but he had a job and nearly a full head of hair—and like Mama said, "That's nothing to sneeze on."

MANAGING BUBBIE

We always manage to come back to the same discussions, Bubbie and me. I know she means well in her own nutty "Yiddishe- bubbie-on-a-mission-from-hell" sort of way, but sometimes you've just got to take control of a situation. I remember a couple of years ago, Bubbie was hospitalized again with some complication or another. The machines were beeping. The nurses were scampering. The morphine was kicking. Bubbie was semiconscious on a wobbly aluminum hospital bed. The oxygen tubes in her nose made her look like she was being attacked by the brain-sucking alien from the Saturday morning Creature Feature. Yet, through it all, we struggled to communicate. I remember that our hazy conversation went something like this:

Me:

Bubbie, how you feeling? They say you came through the surgery like a champ.

The machines and Bubbie wheezed in harmony.

Bubbie:

All right. I'm still here. A little tired—but still here.

Me:

You're supposed to be tired, Bubbie. You just had open-heart surgery.

Bubbie:

Ach, open-heart surgery. Vat open-heart surgery? Ten thousand dollars they charge me! That vas no open-heart surgery—that vas open-pocket surgery! I hear the nurses say to the doctor—"Hey, Doctor, vhat's she got?" I'll tell you vhat she's got—money!

Me:

Bubbie, don't you worry about that. Just be happy that you're okay and with your family.

Bubbie:

Ach, I know, you're right. I shouldn't get aggravated mit these people. Listen, never mind the doctors.

She taps the back of my hand firmly and points at me with her middle finger.

Bubbie:

I have something important I vant to talk to you about, Russel, very important. I need you should listen. You're a big boy now, in college, kinehora,* and it's time you should get married. Oy, such blessings that I should live to dance on your wedding.

I try to plead to her old-fashioned sensibilities in a desperate play for time.

Me:

Bubbie, shouldn't I finish school first so I can support—

Bubbie:

This doesn't matter. You're a smart boy. You'll manage, Russel. I know you'll manage. You just listen to your bubbie.

I should realize by now there's nowhere to run.

Me:

All right, Bubbie, let's hear it. Who is she?

---

* Bless you (really, a curse in reverse)

Bubbie:

I tink you should marry my brother's great-granddaughter.

This is why they say matchmaking on morphine is never a good idea.

Me:

Bubbie, I'm not marrying my cousin. We'd have kids with five heads.

Bubbie:

Ach, don't be crazy. She comes from a good Jewish family.

Me:

Bubbie, of course you say it's a good Jewish family—it's your family. Just think of the money we'd save on wedding invitations—only half as many relatives to invite...Bubbie? Bubbie?

I watch as Bubbie is suddenly distracted by the flickering television anchored above her hospital bed. The Oprah Winfrey Show© is just ending, and again she points the middle finger.

Bubbie:

See, she's like you.

I stare fixedly at the television praying she hasn't found yet another long-lost famous relative.

Me:

How do you mean she's like me, Bubbie?

Bubbie:

She has a nice man, Oprah, and she don't vant to marry him. Vat's the matter mit her?

Me:

Maybe she's not ready yet.

Bubbie:

*Ach, that's crazy. He's nice looking, and I seen
on the television that he writes books. You know,
they make a lot of money—these book writers. She
vouldn't even have to vork no more if she married
him.*

She may be the only person in America with that particular spin
on the Oprah/Stedman romance.

Me:

*Bubbie, I kinda think she does okay on her own.
You know, with that TV show and all.*

Bubbie:

*Vell, I tink it's crazy. Who vants to struggle so
much if you can stay home and take care on a
family? All mine life, I had to vork. There vas never
nobody to take care on me and mine children. All
right, listen, I shouldn't complain—I managed. But
it vould have been nice. Mine life vasn't easy, you
know.*

Me:

I know, Bubbie. I know the stories.

Her eyes widen and suddenly, for just a moment, she's back.

Bubbie:

*You been writing these tings vhat I tell you? Mine
stories—you write them down?*

Me:

Yeah, Bubbie, I write it. I write it all down.

She smiles half-crooked through wires and tubes then reaches
again for my hand.

Bubbie:
Good, ve gonna make a ton of money, you and me.
You listen vhat I tell you about these book writers.
This Oprah's no dummy. Now go on—invite your
cousin for dinner.

Managing Bubbie is a delicate game. It's like working a puppet
with a thousand strings. And sometimes—just sometimes—I won-
der which of us is tugging them.

CHAPTER V
A STITCH IN TIME

···

They set up a small tailor shop below their row-house duplex in Brussels. Jacob made suits. Lea hemmed dresses. Esther went back to Poland. Her work was done.

Life in Belgium was good, and the business boomed. Before long, their little store had a crew of seamstresses churning out men's suits. Jacob's craft was fast becoming the talk of the burgermeisters in the local garment district.

But everything changed with a knock at the door. It was Friday, late. Burned scraps of garlic-roasted rabbit and mashed potatoes soaked in murky dishwater. The radio hummed with static as Jacob dozed on the couch. Another middle-class floral-print living room was at peace. Jacob's younger brother, Avram, stood humbly at the door, back from another failed business venture in Turkey or Morocco or some other arid country where Jews are violently unwelcome. A family had finally settled him—a little boy and a pretty Galitzian girl with a big pregnant belly. Perhaps things really were different now.

August 12, 1929

My dearest Evelyn,

Here is my latest news. Jacob's brother has moved in. He finally gave up wandering the world and making revolutions with the communists and—if you'd believe it—settled down with a wife and son. Of course, right after he found a wife, he found our doorstep. So here they are. He's without a job, and she's Galitzian and pregnant with another baby. Oy, Evelyn, she makes me crazy. You know how these Galitzians know everything. All day long, she has to remind everybody how educated she is and how uneducated we are. And you know Jacob, he can't say no to anyone—especially his brother. So he made him a partner in the business. Avram sells the suits, while me and Jacob do the work and make them. The wife, like the rest of the Galitzians, just supervises. Oy, Evelyn you couldn't imagine the tumult. Last month, I see that suits are going out, but no money is coming in, so I ask her how this could be. She says to me, "I made a deal with the Bon Marché store. They pay for the suits once they sell them." Well, I know this is crazy, so I tell her we need to get the money now, and she says, "Oh, dear, you're not an educated woman. You couldn't possibly understand these things, and I don't have time to explain it to you." So, I let her have it, and the next morning I go to Jacob that he should discuss this problem with Avram. It takes him two days to get the nerve to speak with him, but they finally worked it out like brothers. They punched each other's teeth out. Oy, such a mess! Evelyn, I thought we were going to lose everything from this, and Jacob's heart was broken about his brother, but things are getting a little better. We've started selling suits again, and I know Jacob sneaks out sometimes to the pub to see Avram, so at least he's happy again. Let me know all is well in America. Maybe we'll come to you there if things don't pick up soon. But I know Jacob will bounce back on his feet.

All my love,
Lea

—m—

Just as she figured, the business boomed, and the family blossomed. And by 1931, Lea had given birth to a baby girl. They named her Faygal, in memory of Aunt Faygala—the plain woman with all the diamonds. But to the Belgians, she would be Fanny.

Lea had never seen Jacob so happy. He showered her with presents and attention and even bought her a two-carat diamond ring. Lea was speechless. Jacob wasn't the sort to lavish gifts. He had done nothing like that for her birthday or their anniversary. But this time was special. She had given him a child, and soon after, a second child. Her name was Eva.

The children grew up like Belgians. Fanny was her father's girl— dark-haired and olive-skinned. She was a sensible child who liked to knit. Eva was different. Radiant and rosy, lace and bows. Eva danced. To the ends of the earth, she'd dance. Until the sun went down, she'd dance and never stop—a marionette waiting to spring from her music box.

Sometimes it seemed as though life could go on like that forever— sunny skies, a busy shop, and Sunday market days at the People's Bakery where Jacob and the girls would spend hours eating chocolate-covered caramels and Baba au Rhum pastries so juicy that the rum would pour from the paper bags all over their new clothes and soak their mother's fresh-cleaned floor. And Lea would get so angry, she'd shout, "Damn it, Jacob! Must I spend my whole life cleaning up after you?" These were the problems of nineteen-thirties Belgium—a peaceful, pastry bliss.

CHAPTER VI
A FOOL'S FOLLY

···

Jacques Edelstein was an idiot. And maybe Jacob was just as bad for following him. Jacques was a tall, pencil-shaped pelt peddler with a shrubby moustache and curly black hair that launched in all directions—only to eventually, miraculously, form a perfect basketball-shaped Afro. He'd come around the shop on Wednesdays, pushing a rusty grocery wagon filled with swatches of unfinished leather—"The finest in Spain. Feel that texture—it's like a baby's ass. And you know, my friend, for you I always make a special price"—which was somehow always five francs higher than the next guy's price. But Jacob liked him. Jacob liked everyone. Maybe that's what got him in trouble.

I guess he should have known it. Nothing that starts with "I've got a plan that's going to make us buckets of money" ever ends well. But how could he say no? Lea had tried for years to teach him, but somehow he never seemed to learn. Jacob was just the sort who'd give you the shirt off his back and, if you asked him right, stitch you the pants to match. So it was no wonder he stumbled straight into trouble.

"Jacob, my wise friend, I'm going to let you in on the opportunity of a lifetime. Listen close," the lanky peddler puffed, knowing well that Jacob always listened to anyone he wasn't married to. "These poodles in Paris—these rich women who do nothing but shop all day—will pay three hundred francs for a fine winter coat with a fox-fur collar. I hear the Bon Marché has the stones to charge three fifty. All we need to do is make the same coats cheaper, stand outside their store, and sell them for two fifty. We'll make a killing."

Of course, Jacob managed to get about five steps across the border before he was quickly arrested by French authorities. Trespass and theft of design was, I think, the official charge. The Parisians took few offenses more seriously than crimes against fashion. Bail was 2,000 francs, and Jacques was gone—with the merchandise. As usual, Lea was there by morning to clean up his mess.

—ℳ—

But life went on, and the family stitched along, though things in Europe were darkening like a menacing cloud floating in from the far horizon. By 1936, rumors of trouble across the frontier in Germany were rampant. A stringy-haired chancellor had seized power, and politics were changing fast. Newspapers touted a wave of race laws designed to preserve the purity of the German Nation. Radios trumpeted the Nazi Party's proud new commitment to resolving Germany's Jewish Problem. You could feel them beneath your skin—creeping closer, growing stronger. Still, for most, this was no cause for concern—another fascist government flexing its muscle against another ethnic minority. But to those who had survived the pogroms in Russia and Poland, the signs were troubling—the jagged tip of a much bigger iceberg. They knew well how that sort handled their ethnic problems.

But the Gestapo, the curfews, and that shattered-glass world of Berlin, all seemed so far from Brussels—tidbits from the fish-wrap section of the Sunday news. Belgium wasn't like that. Belgium was modern. Belgium was liberal. Belgium was safe.

So the world went on with the more pressing business of pension cuts and bus strikes, while gradually the stories of unruly neighbors crept closer to the front pages. Each article unveiled a greater menace:

GERMANS RESUME PRODUCTION OF WEAPONS.

REVITALIZED BERLIN TO HOST OLYMPIC GAMES.

LEBENSRAUM FOR HITLER IN CZECHOSLOVAKIA.

Then, in September 1939, on the icy stoop of her bustling shop, Lea read an incredible headline—the sort you have to glance at a few times before the words actually take shape and sink in. A 64-point print cried—**WAR! Hitler Invades Poland!**

Lea raced out a letter to her mother. Surely she must have left when word got out that the Germans were coming? For months, Lea waited with no response, no word of what happened to her family in Poland. Then, in November, a note from Evelyn explained the story.

November 13, 1939

My dearest Lea,

I hope you, Jacob and the children are well. I am worried about Mama. Abe says she is still in Poland. When the war broke out, Abe took everyone to Russia on his motorcycle—better Stalin than Hitler, he figured. Each night for a week he schlepped back and forth across the border on the motorcycle—first with Malcha, then the kids, then Malcha's ten brothers and sisters—all of them. But Mama wouldn't go. She said she had no interest in living with the wolves and communists in Siberia. Why must she always be so stubborn? Have you heard anything from her? On the radio, they say the Jews are put in ghettos. Please write soon to let me know she is well.

All My Love,

Evelyn

PS—The lawyers gave me these affidavits for you to fill out so you can get the visa to come here to America.

Months passed, and still no news of Esther. Rumors swirled about ghettos and camps, but no one knew where she was, or whether she was all right. Friends from Lodz who had fled to Russia heard that Isaac had also stayed behind. One thing was for certain—if those two were together, the Germans had more than one war on their hands.

—⁓—

Back in Belgium, panicked Jews were racing to learn all they could about the ones still trapped in the old country. And while Belgium's king promised protection for all his subjects, anyone with a hand in the old country still worried.

Only the children seemed unmoved. Poland was a history book. They were Belgians, raised and groomed in the French culture of their birthland. Their life, their world, their language—all were French. They didn't dwell on ties to Poland or crusty old Jews a million miles away. Belgium was home.

But things had changed in Brussels. Europe was at war, and conflict was creeping closer. Rumors were spinning that it was just a matter of time before blitzkrieg would rain on Belgium. People were scared and leaving in droves. Lea and her family hoped to stay forever, but she knew too well that Europe would never be safe. Nervous Jews were telling thirdhand stories of horrors that were being committed in Poland and Germany—stories of families being dragged from their homes at gun-point in the middle of the night; stories of children being trampled by rock-hurling mobs; other tales too awful to believe.

Whatever was happening over there, one thing was clear—Belgium wasn't safe. Lea resolved to join her sister in the United States and quickly began inquiring about travel permits. She contacted a lawyer, who contacted another lawyer, who contacted yet another. They were no help to her, these lawyers, always talking to themselves, so she decided to take matters into her own hands. She marched downtown, shuffling from government office to government office battling bureaucrats who pointed her from one line to the next. She sent document after document, only to receive responses requesting more paperwork. All the while, German forces drew closer.

By this point the Belgians had started gearing up for war. Tool factories now churned out weapons; textile mills belched uniforms and parachutes by the thousands. In town, women were recruited to man the assembly lines, while the men were drafted to fight. To avoid the Belgian draft, Jacob agreed to enlist with the French forces—better to go with the bigger army, he figured, though the sly little tailor had no intention of ever fighting for anyone.

—∞—

On May 10, 1940, the inevitable day came. The Nazis invaded Belgium. They took it with little effort. The Belgian forces were ill equipped to fight the German war machine. Axis troops moved so swiftly that the bombers seemed to reach the capital before word of the invasion had even spread. Buildings crumbled in flashes of fire and clouds of dust as the radio finally broadcast news of the attack. By that point, Brussels was in panic, and the white flag was flying.

The city was in chaos. German troops goose-stepped in thunderous rhythm. Machine guns rained victory blasts above the city square as red-and-black swastikas fluttered in the wind. Hysterical mobs, harried from the frenzy, hurried for the nearest trains out of town. From the north, sirens screamed atop echoing bombs as Lea directed her family's escape.

"Grab a few satchels, and fill them with food and warm clothes!" she cried as she tucked her savings and diamond ring in her blouse. The Nazis marched right past their porch as she ushered the children through the doorway into the mad rush of people. In their wake, a pot of chicken soup bubbled and simmered on a new yellow stove. The radio chattered the hour's news a little late. A pink scarf, a Mother's Day surprise that Fanny had been knitting for Mama, lay buried in the crevices of the couch. A lifetime's memories left frozen in the moment.

"Take only what you can carry, Come on, girls. Go! Go!" Lea barked as they scurried to the alleyway. The door never even closed behind them. It didn't matter. They knew they were never coming back.

—◇—

Streets and avenues were a swirling sea of bodies pushing and screaming the names of loved ones lost in the shuffle. Children cried for missing mothers. Dogs sniffed nervously for families long gone. The cauldron called Europe had boiled over.

Hearts racing, they trampled the shards of a world they once knew, racing desperately through the mob and rubble toward the train station at Midi. En route, Jacob panicked. "I can't do this, Lea, I want to go back to the apartment. Maybe if I surrender myself peacefully, it won't be so bad."

They both knew better. She had to gain control of the situation. "Jacob, this is it—right here, right now—our only chance. You've heard the stories, seen the letters. You know what will happen if we stay. If this is our day to die, then so be it, but I won't die hiding in a corner waiting for my executioner."

So Jacob followed Lea and the children, more because she had ahold of his hair than on account of her inspirational words, but at least they were on their way.

By the time they reached the train depot, thousands were in line. Lea could hardly believe it. Bombers were on the brink of leveling the entire city, and these sheep were waiting for tickets. Unwilling to stand idle with the herd, she grabbed Jacob and the children and shoved them into an open cab at the back of the train. The railway workers were too busy selling tickets to the howling masses to notice a few stowaways.

So the young family quietly took their seats at the back of the train and tried to act as if they were supposed to be there. It was a rule Jewish refugees learned quickly—look like you belong, and people will believe that you do. Through the smoky window of the departing train, they watched as the huge crowd of people lingered idly at the station—still waiting for their tickets. For a while, the trip was as uneventful as a train ride can be in the middle of a blitzkrieg. Luckily, at this point the Germans were more interested in bombing the city than attacking a caravan of refugees. An hour—maybe two—ticked by to the steady chug of the steam engine, until eventually, the train crept into the French border station.

—∿∿—

Leave it to the French to finally find something that they could do swiftly and efficiently. Within minutes, they had sorted everyone who didn't have French citizenship or travel papers and began directing them to a train back to Belgium. Jacob started to tremble as the soldiers ordered him and his family to the Brussels-bound train.

But Lea refused to go. Remembering Jacob's promise to enlist with the French army, she quickly grabbed his military registration documents and waved them in front of a soldier. All the papers said in five or six pages was that Jacob was exempt from joining the Belgian army because he planned to join the French army, but at times like that, you work with what you've got.

"See these papers?" she barked. "The French government has brought my husband all the way from Belgium to come fight for your army, and you don't want to let him in. Do you think they bring just anybody all the way from Belgium to defend your country?"

The guard looked puzzled as he tried to figure what important military purpose this tiny shivering man could serve. He started to review the papers, but they were long and wordy, and he quickly bored of pretending to read. There was a seal on them, and that seemed official enough. Jacob and his family were escorted back to the Paris-bound train with apologies. The French may have had a big army, but fortunately, it wasn't a smart one.

TO SUE OR NOT TO SUE

The conversation with my grandmother veers from personal to professional. Like every other college kid from this neighborhood, I'm studying law, which to her makes me "a learned boy" and, therefore, uniquely qualified to answer questions about anything from TV repair to medicine. Today, luckily, it's a little closer to my chosen field.

Bubbie:

I vant you should listen to this. I have a big case for you.

Maybe an accident on the bus, a slip and fall in the pharmacy...To be honest, I couldn't imagine what she was driving at.

Bubbie:

I vant you should sue Ed McMahon for me.

This I gotta hear.

Me:

Okay, Bubbie, why do you want to sue Ed McMahon?

Bubbie:

Look on this, vat he sends me, this Ed Schmuckman!

She rummages through her bag, dumping watermelon candies and wrinkled Kleenex onto the Formica coffee table until finally, she finds her letter.

Bubbie:

See, look here! This says "LEA LAZEGA, YOU'RE THE NEXT TEN MILLION DOLLARS VINNER."
He tells me I won ten million dollars—Right there.

See, there's mine name, and there's his face! And it says, "Lea Lazega, you're a vinner." How could they let him send such a tings? I vas so excited, I vas dancing in the halls. The whole condominium looked on me like I vas crazy. I vas dancing a waltz with my ninety-year-old neighbor—oy, mit her walker—and we vere singing, "If I vere a rich man, ya di deedle"—you know this song from Fiddler on the Roof? Well anyvay, they tell me now that this is—how do you call it?—bullshit!

Me:
Bubbie, he sends these things to everyone.

Bubbie:
Vell, this is not right. I vant you should make a lawsuit on him.

Me:
I can't sue Ed McMahon, I'm not even a lawyer yet.

I thought it was a rock-solid excuse.

Bubbie:
This doesn't matter. You're a very smart boy. You can make this case for me.

I could just picture the scene, "Well, Judge, I'm not quite a member of the bar yet, but my bubbie thinks I'm bright enough to champion her cause." Time to switch to plan B.

Me:
I'll tell you what. I don't think we have much of a case, you know, on account of the Republicans and the new Game Show Host Protection Act...

(In my house it's always a safe bet to blame your misfortunes on conservative politicians—except for President Reagan, of course, what with him being family and all.)

Me:

But, Bubbie, if you're that upset, maybe we can organize a family-wide boycott of Ed McMahon stuff.

Bubbie:

Vill this make him pay me my ten million dollars?

Me:

Probably not, but I think it's the best we can do.

A moment of desperate anticipation ticks by as I anxiously gauge her deliberate reaction. Is she buying it? An eyebrow raises. The head nods ever so slightly...Going...Going...

Bubbie:

Oy, my grandson, the lawyer, such a smart boy!

Sold!

So it was done—sealed with a slobbery mothball kiss that I couldn't wipe from my forehead fast enough. Star Search was off limits, the Colonial Penn life insurance was canceled, and Ed McMahon became persona non grata in our home. Understand, sometimes it's better to just roll with a raging tide than to fight it head on.

CHAPTER VII
WE'LL ALWAYS HAVE PARIS

···

The family eventually arrived in Paris to the shadow of *La Tour Eiffel* and the comforting home of friends. Like so many who had fled Belgium, Jacob and the children never dreamed that mighty France could ever fall. This was France, after all—the mother of fashion and the cradle of culture. The Germans wouldn't dare. They couldn't. Not this soon. Not yet.

But governments tumble, and map lines move. And Lea was sure that, like so much these days, the peace wouldn't last long—even in the City of Lights. At the end of the day even the grand Eiffel Tower was just nuts and bolts that could come unraveled with the right mix of force and determination.

So unpacking was forbidden. It would only slow them down when it came time to run again. They wore what they had, and what they had, stunk: onion-peel layers of gray wool sweaters and heavy winter coats stained with the marks of the mayhem around them. There had hardly even been a moment for a bath since Brussels.

But Jacob, the blissful optimist, of course saw sunshine. "Lea, would you settle down?" He gently promised, "We're safe here. This isn't like Belgium. The French have a big army. They'll never let Paris be taken."

Lea had seen enough of the French army to know that was no reassurance.

Despite all that had happened in Belgium, the French really believed that Paris was untouchable. Paris was somehow special—sacred. Even the girls were at home. They dreamed in the glow of the bright city lights and soaked in the sweet smell of baguettes baking on the cobblestone street below.

So Lea burrowed in and bode her time until she could find somewhere else to go. The truth was that Jacob and the others were right. For now, Paris was the safest place. Even if Hitler could beat the French, it wouldn't be quick. Surely, they could never storm Paris the way they had Brussels. Surely there'd be time.

So they settled and began planning their next steps. The first job was to get French residency papers. Jacob's worthless military documents would only go so far before some industrious soldier actually decided to read them.

Early one morning, with Jacob and the children in tow, Lea marched down to the *préfecture*. The complex consisted of four green-roofed Parisian-style buildings set in a square. Simple, yet functional, the design eased the process of spinning aggrieved citizens in circles. All day she bounced from one building to the next, collecting one official stamp after another. At each stop, some paper-puncher would complain of some critical missing seal from another department in another building. Round and round the circle again. The French obsession with bureaucratic red tape was matched only by the Germans'.

One good thing about spending your days wandering government offices, though, is you are the first to hear official gossip. Bureau girls were chirping about German encroachment around the Maginot line. Whatever that meant, it couldn't be good.

Like a tumbling avalanche set in motion, service counter windows slammed shut booth by booth like a chain of cascading dominos. Confused clerks raced out the back to a public bus idling in the alley, while oblivious patrons waited in line, complaining of obnoxious delays and squandered taxes.

Lea and the family quietly followed outside where an unwitting bus driver sat comfortably perched on the steps of his new ride, enjoying a quick smoke before his next run. The bureaucrats swarmed the driver, negotiations ensued, and before long it was settled—the driver would evacuate whatever city staff he could fit on his bus. "Take care of your own." It was the sworn creed of the French civil service.

As for Lea, she wasn't about to wait for another opportunity. These people had a bus, and she was getting on it. She grabbed Jacob and the kids and followed the clerks onto their ticket out of town. "Remember, just walk on there like you know where you are going," she reminded them. Some may have noticed the young family trembling at the front of the bus, but what did they care? They all had their seats, and before anyone knew it, the bus was on its way.

—⁊⁊⁊—

It must have been noon when they finally reached a bustling train station on the outskirts of Paris. In the background, they could hear the crowd and the fighting draw closer—the chatter and screams of a panicked mob, gradually smothered by the reverberating blasts of approaching bombs.

Mother, children, and tailor lumbered down the steel steps to bedlam as panicked refugees shouted and shook papers at befuddled railway clerks. Like lost sheep, the herd again waited for tickets. It was as if they were holding onto normal in a world that had forgotten the word. But Lea knew to wait for no one.

She followed the bureaucrats to an idle train and hovered impatiently, anxiously tapping her feet as if just a little extra nudge would start them moving. She tapped. She paced. She drummed her fingers on the pine bench seats. But nothing worked. They were still stranded and out of time. At the foot of the aisle, a hefty porter pushed his belly through the crowd barking "Journalists and Americans! Journalists and Americans! Exit now. Your train is on the north tracks." Americans and journalists—surely their fate had to be better than Gypsies, Jews, and bureaucrats waiting for a ride to nowhere. Instinctively, she grabbed her family and raced toward it. She knew only one thing—"Anywhere but here."

At the north-side tracks a silver passenger car waited open and unguarded. Slowly, they slunk inside...steadily, warily...until a gentle voice called from behind, "Papier, *madame?*" Her heart stopped beating. "*Papier, madame, si vous plait*—ticket, please, ma'am," the voice repeated. An observant porter had seen them crossing.

Lea's thoughts froze as she stared blankly into his pale gray eyes. The end of the line, it seemed, was near. She inhaled deeply and started to speak, "We..." She grasped for a lie, but the porter didn't need one. He lifted a finger to his lips and breathed a quiet "shhhh," whispering softly as he waved them aboard, "I have a family, too. Go on. I didn't see you." Paris fast became a memory as the screaming alarms of a world going to hell slowly faded in the distance.

The train continued to inch safely away from the city as people slowly settled into their railcars. There was no ticket; no schedule; no destination. She knew only that they were headed west, far from the advancing troops.

By now the crowd had begun to settle. Breathless gasps at last found air as the train cleared the fringe of the city and drew distance from the attack. For a moment there was calm as concrete fast faded to country-side. But soon again, the invasion alarm wailed.

Bombers were making a run at the train. The bantering passengers chilled to a numb silence as the baritone hum of approaching aircrafts echoed in their eardrums. They could feel the vibrations of the race as it quickly intensified—a buzzing chorus of Luftwaffe Stukas gaining on a struggling steam engine. The drum of the locomotive chugged deeply as it fought to make its escape. From the sound of things, the train was losing. The drone of descending attack crafts grew louder until it was right on top of them—BOOM! Then again—BOOM! And then again—BOOM! The train shrieked as it strained to grip its tracks. It managed to hold the rail but the last four cars were demolished. Dozens were dead. Hundreds were wounded. Bodies were strewn in all directions. Miraculously, the rest of the train remained intact. The luggage and anything else that wasn't bolted down was tossed about the compartment, but the car was, somehow, in one piece.

In a restless frenzy, the passengers struggled to get their bearings and find their families. Through the smoke, Lea could see the silhouettes of her husband and Eva—they were shaken, but alive. She called out to Fanny. There was no response.

CHAPTER VIII
QUIET MIRACLES

························

Lea fumbled through the wreckage, hunting frantically for her little girl, but the smoke made the search nearly impossible. She cried out again, in desperation, "Fanny? Fanny?" No answer. She tried clearing the luggage that had tumbled from the overhead compartments—still no sign of her. Then there, beneath the seat, they found her, curled and shaking. She had taken shelter under one of those old wood benches. They were uncomfortable as hell, but rock solid. The windows along the loading side of the train were shattered from the force of the explosion. Desperately, Lea brushed the bits of broken glass from her daughter's cheek, crying hysterically over and over again, "Are you okay, baby? Are you okay?"

Fanny just stared at her mother, speechless, as Lea wiped the tiny trails of blood from the tips of her cheeks. All the while, no one ever realized that Fanny wasn't responding. For now, it was enough that she wasn't holding her baby's lifeless body. She lugged Fanny to a big-nosed American, a reporter, who had a first-aid kit and was bandaging wounded. He started by dressing his own injuries. A suitcase had fallen and broken his nose. Lea was hardly surprised. "With a nose like that—how could it miss?"

Their wounds treated, they set out for safety. It wouldn't be long before the Germans would search for survivors. They set off in no particular direction. Everyone had scattered different ways, though no one seemed to know where they were heading. Lea figured it was best they separate. A handful of wandering refugees would be tougher to spot than a hundred.

Like most, they eventually made their way to an armory on the edge of town, where hundreds slept on mattresses of straw and waited for bodies to be cleared and the train to be put right. Then, by morning, it was done. Half a train was headed somewhere. At this point, where just didn't seem to matter.

—⁘—

For the entire trip, Fanny said nothing, she just stared with a glazed look in her eyes. She wasn't responding to voices, to sounds, to anything. Lea feared she'd stay like that forever—deaf and dumb. For three nights, Lea prayed at her bedside that her daughter would snap out of her stupor. "Lord, I know your angels looked after us on that train, and I should be ashamed to even ask for another miracle, but please, I beg you, give me back my daughter."

On the fourth night, the angels answered. Fanny's eyes twinkled with life as she gently tugged at her mother's dress. "I can hear, Mama. With this ear, I can hear."

Lea fell to her knees and cried. The angels had sheltered them from the bombs and given her daughter back her hearing. Even if only one ear could hear, that was still enough of a miracle.

TWO ROADS DIVERGED IN A WOOD
AND SHE SAID TO HELL
WITH BOTH OF THEM

Bubbie is a survivor. She has made her way by ignoring conventional wisdom and following her own path. Right now that path has taken her back to the couch, where she can sit for a while. Up and down—back and forth—can be exhausting at that age. My uncle, Stanley, has joined us. He greets every living creature with an honest smile and a glowing compliment.

Stanley:
Lea, you look wonderful. I love that dress.

Bubbie:
Oy, thank you, Stanley. It vas a lot of aggravation to make this dress. Ach, such a fight I had mit that tailor because of this clothes. I come to him, and I say, "I vant you should make a little shorter the hemline and a little bit wider the hips." This tailor makes the hips so big like for the tuchas from an elephant. Ach, such a mess. So I tell him, "Oh, no, I von't pay for such a ting. I vant I should take it to another tailor." And this tailor has the chutzpah—the nerve—to say to me he von't give the dress unless I pay him. Oy, have you ever seen such a tings? So, I say to him I'm going to call my grandson, the lawyer, that he should make a case on you. And he says, "Oh, yeah, vell my son's a lawyer, too, and I'm going to make a lawsuit on you." This, I don't tolerate, so I tell him, "Vell, you listen to me, mister, I have two grandsons are

*lawyers and a granddaughter a judge. You don't
vant from the kind of trouble I can make you."*

Three lawyers to one. Do the math—she's got him beat hands
down.

Stanley:
So, did he fix the dress?

Bubbie:
*Ach, finally, after I fight maybe an hour mit that
tailor, he says, "Okay, lady, I fix the dress for you—
no charge." Ach, who needs such aggravations?
But I have to stand up for what's right. I know from
good tailoring.*

Bubbie's not an easy customer. She has waddled through life on
raw tenacity and an unbending refusal to do as she's told—it's an
instinct that's always served her well.

CHAPTER IX
BRETAGNE

....

Last stop—End of the line. Bretagne, France, was where they finally finished, a quiet place of tall pine and hard gray granite softly flanking the eastern edge of the English Channel. For now, it was time to rest—time to settle.

Anxious civilians struggled to situate as military caravans retreated across His Majesty's choppy channel. On the shores of Cherbourg, the British newsmen said stay put—victory was at hand. But London radio lied. Your own eyes told you the Germans were winning, and France was falling.

An unfriendly flag flew high over Paris, and refugees flooded what remained of the unoccupied world. Housing was scarce. Relief lines stretched halfway to Holland. Hotels quartered only the highest bidders. Still, government agencies peddled worthless advice about far-off places said to be safe and accommodating. July 1940 was a time of locked doors and closed hearts. The world, it seemed, had its own problems.

That was all just as well. Lea could do for herself if she could just find someone in the know.

But Rue de Siam had no answers, just a cop—a baby-faced patrolman who'd heard something about a tiny farm just south of Caen where a group of refugees had recently settled. For now, that would have to do.

—◊—

The small farm fronted a long lonely road far from the fringe of the city, in a place that seemed to spill off the edge of the earth. Just a narrow path of hard-pressed dirt led the way to a wondrous new world of trees, grass, and open spaces. It was a place where rolling greens stretched straight to the horizon and wild horses grazed along the open roadside. All that showed of people was the occasional pitch-roofed house of pine and stone that dotted the distant landscape.

As for the farm, it was ragged—even by wartime standards. Abandoned machinery littered unplowed fields. Skinny animals with shabby coats roamed a patchy pasture penned by untrimmed hedges and rusted chicken wire. A small stone-rimmed well was filled with mud, so sun-browned girls rinsed long black curls in rainwater that poured from the sloping tin rooftop. They say it had never rained like it did in July 1940 in Bretagne.

In the sopping fields, rain-soaked men eyed huddled cattle, hoping to choose the best for milking. It was just a matter of catching the slowest one, they figured.

Lea watched in wonder. "They put these Jews on a farm?" There was a music teacher, a rabbinical student, a history professor, and, of course, no one who could do something as useful as slaughter food and cook it. "So many geniuses, and these guys were trying to figure out which part of a bull to milk." Lea was baffled. "Don't Jews ever teach their children anything handy? Oy, I hope they don't think we're gonna grow our own food. We'll starve."

Fortunately, the French government didn't believe in a Jewish green thumb either, so they provided vouchers for food and basic provisions. The women would take the vouchers into town and haul back rice and *le lait condense*, while the men stayed busy milking the bulls and debating Europe's greater problems.

Rations were regular, but always slim. Priority went first to native French and then to refugee children. So they pooled what they had, and between them they had enough for a couple cups of rice, a baguette, and a bit of milk—once a day. It was a lumpy, condensed milk that they'd pour all over the rice—"to make the children strong."

—⟋⟍—

Tuesday, July 9, 1940. Mail call again. Mail was delivered in town, which was a quaint little village about a million miles from nowhere. There was just one letter that day. It was from an old neighbor in Brussels. The page felt a thousand pounds heavy.

June 12, 1940

Dear Lea,

I have awful news from Avram. After you left, things got desperate here in Brussels. Germans with lists were everywhere, kicking down doors and taking people away. All night you could hear the screams—awful screams—and gunshots all around. They came last week for Avram, but he saw them through the window and went up to the roof to hide. But Franya insisted she could solve the situation, because she could speak German with the soldier. But that only made things worse, so she tried hitting him on the head with a frying pan. Oh, Lea, the screams, those children. He shot her in the head, right there in her kitchen, in front of her babies. Then, finally, thank G-d, he ran away, just a boy afraid of what he'd done. Anyway, for now we must hide. But whatever you do, you must never come back. Each day gets worse. Joseph and I bought fake papers, and first chance we get we will leave to Jerusalem.

Stay well,

Rivka

Lea braced both hands to the table as she read the letter. She knew right then that, no matter what, she could never let it happen to her. "I wasn't so educated like Franya, but I knew. You don't negotiate, you don't fight—you just run as fast and far as you can."

After the tragedy, Avram took the children and hid each one with a different Catholic family. It broke his heart to think that his children wouldn't be Jewish, but he understood that five thousand years of heritage and tradition is a modest price to save your children.

—⁓—

Thursday, October 24, 1940, was just a mail run like any other until the bombs fell. It all came about so swiftly. Firestorms rained from the sky. Great green tanks blasted all that stood. Desperate civilians scurried for cover, shouting names of those who had fallen behind. The soul of France had been hijacked.

In the midst of it all, Lea raced back to the farm. She had to warn them to run. She had to get her family. But by then word had come. French police had arrived with a German official and posted an order that "all Jews were to gather their things and register for volunteer labor." The philosophizing farmers debated what next. Not Lea. She wasn't about to sign her name to some German list. "Better to try for a transit visa."

At that time, Belgian papers said nothing about religion, and the Nazis would be looking for what you were—not what you weren't. So it was decided to go.

Of course, Jacob had reservations. "Lea, you go on and get the permits, and I'll stay and watch the children." There was no way she was going to leave her children on that farm—the husband, he could stay and wait for the Gestapo, but not the children. The only choice was to keep moving. With each child tightly in hand, she set off down the long unbending road to town.

The village was a picture of wartime carnage—houses, shops, and churches were now little more than piles of wood and broken rock littering the cobblestone streets. The Nazis rolled through the tiny town with the same swiftness and precision that they used to level it. A cavalcade of tanks crushed a path through the debris for goose-stepping soldiers rhythmically stomping at their tail. Along the dusty curbside, bewildered onlookers gazed in disbelief as they watched their homes and memories trampled by the parading troops. In the wake of the procession, a puzzled yellow dog sniffed anxiously through the rubble, desperately in search of his master. Above it all, Hitler's bloodred banners—with their twisted black crosses—fluttered triumphantly as if to say, "Look what we have wrought." The devil himself had visited Bretagne.

The devil had leveled the church, so the only place big enough to house the Gestapo was an old schoolhouse across from the butcher. The Nazis entrenched themselves so swiftly and smoothly, you'd have thought that the occupation had always been. Everywhere, there were signs and guards directing people where to go. Outside the school, a formidable crowd gathered to register for "Jewish Volunteer Labor."

"Work hard, and you will be rewarded," promised the men with machine guns who ushered volunteers at gunpoint to wood-penned cattle cars. Lea and the children cleared the Jewish line and slipped midway into the school when a stone-faced soldier stopped them. "*Papieren. Papieren,*" he demanded. He was cold and unflinching. She pretended not to understand. "Papier," the soldier barked in French, shaking a fist full of papers beneath her chin.

An unsteady hand surrendered four well-used Belgian passports. The guard studied his list and then the papers. There was nothing of interest to him. He inspected them carefully for any sign of Jewishness—a name, a religious designation. There was none. She drew breath and explained that they had fled the attack on Brussels, and since France had been blown to bits, they just wanted to go home.

"You bombed us in Belgium, so we left," she told him. "Now that you bombed us here, what difference does it make? We might as well go back." Her seamless fib made perfect sense. The guard agreed to issue the permit but would need to see Jacob first.

"You don't know what a flu he has," she cried. "You wouldn't wish on your worst enemy such a sickness, and you want I should make him walk all the way here?"

The soldier wasn't budging. "No husband, no papers," he answered and quickly returned to his business.

Irate and determined to get those transit permits, Lea stormed back though the soot and rubble to fetch her husband. He was busy packing his things for the labor camp, as ordered. She grabbed his ear and dragged him off the farm. "We are getting on a train away from here and going to America," she informed him.

Jacob laughed. "What train are you going to sneak us on to that will take us to America?" Her scowling look quickly made clear how serious she was. "We'll get the permits to go to Belgium."

"Belgium!" Jacob cried, "Lea, are you crazy? We can't go back there."

"Jacob, just listen," she gently reassured him. "We get the papers to go to Belgium. This train to Belgium goes through unoccupied territories. All we need to do is get on the train, slip off, and run to Toulouse, Marseille, anywhere. Just remember, you have the flu."

Jacob protested, but the decision was made. They were leaving. The whole way into town, his eyes never strayed from the broken and bloodied shards that laid a dusty path to the Gestapo. The closer he got, the more his hands shook from the panic.

Lea tried to settle him as they approached the stone-faced soldier. "Breathe. Take deep breaths, and remember—you've got the flu." She nudged him forward to the guard, who was now busy sorting Jews and other undesirables for the camp-bound cattle cars.

"*Du, komst hier*! You, come here!" the soldier ordered, pointing the way with the machine gun strapped to his shoulder. Jacob inched closer, took one look at the weapon, and again began to quiver. The color drained from his face. There was no time to think. Lea lifted Jacob by the arm. "Do you see what I told you?" she shouted, pushing her shivering ghost of a husband in front of the soldier. "Look at him. He's sick. Very sick. Now, unless you want you should be like him in a couple days, you better let us go, so I can take him to his doctor."

Jacob was convincing. He looked like something worse than the flu. The color had completely fled his face, his teeth chattered, his hands and knees shook, and to top it off, he was already skinny like a pile of bones. The soldier was terrified. He directed them to the front of the line, all the while keeping a healthy distance from the scrawny, quivering man. "Send him to Belgium or wherever the hell he's from. Just get him out of here," the soldier ordered. It wasn't until that very moment that Lea ever truly appreciated having such a sickly looking husband.

SIX DEGREES OF AGGRAVATION

Bubbie's always had this knack for managing things. I think somehow it comes from never having had anyone in life to manage her. I guess maybe that's what also—for a time—made her the mother-in-law from hell for my mom.

I think her "take-charge" personality has just kind of marched her to extremes for her kids—as if, in some not-so-small way, her strength comes from being able to manage everything. Like when my parents first married. They were just a couple of broke teenage hairdressers living in the basement of a Canarsie walk-up—you know, finding their own way like young couples do. Bubbie couldn't bear it. Surely her baby couldn't be getting along like that, she'd rant. So she'd load up her bundles, take three buses across the bridge from the city, walk six Brooklyn blocks in the dead of winter, let herself into the young couple's apartment, and set dinner for one—for my father. He was so skinny, her Maxie. "That girl" couldn't possibly be feeding him—not like her.

Thirty years later, and not much has changed. She's still pushing and schlepping—taking buses to the ends of the earth to get things just her way. She makes rounds about town, hauls an assortment of goodies, and then commandeers my mother's kitchen with packages from Arnie and Richie's and a zillion other places that stink of salmon. "Dahling, I brought you a gefilte fish," she says. "I made it fresh mit a fish from Kosher Kitchen. You know that's my Maxie's favorite—a gefilte fish." After thirty-plus years together, I think Mom knows. "Fresh, not frozen. Don't vorry, I teach you how to make a gefilte fish one day."

I always used to wonder how Mom put up with it, but she kind of gets it. I guess as time passes, and we look back on life, for better or worse, these are the people we remember—the overbearing parent, the third-grade teacher who never let you slouch, the mother-in-law who made you fight for your own. Maybe they're more than just material for us starving writers, and somewhere down the line they make us better—like they leave a mark on us that softens over time but never fades.

CHAPTER X
ALBI

•••••••••••••

Just like she figured, the train drifted into unoccupied territory. They let off near Albi, a forgotten little village in the peaceful shadow of the Cathedral Saint Cecile along the grassy banks of the River Tarn. It was just what they needed to stay discreet, to be invisible.

The first problem was finding food. The money was gone. Anything worth trading or selling had been abandoned long ago. And in those days, there wasn't much use for dirt-poor Jewish refugees. A Jew might work cheap—eight or so francs a day if you were lucky and willing to stow him in your cupboards. But for a little more, you could get a Turk or a Slav with hardly the aggravation, so who'd want to deal with Jews?

So the plan was to start at the synagogue—if there was still a synagogue. It seemed so much of her world was gone or hiding for dear life. But this place was different—so far from the cities and hamlets they had skated through before. It was there in broad daylight for all of the world to see—as if somehow these people were magically able to ignore the havoc around them and calmly read Victor Hugo novels over espresso at *L'Jardin* Café. Albi was beautiful. Albi was peaceful. Albi was oblivious.

October 30, 1940. Finally, someone who knew something about anything. A pretty blond seamstress at the Red Cross had fallen madly in love with a dashing young violinist from Prague and told him a matter to keep in the strictest confidence. The young musician swore twice on all that was dear to him, locked his lips with calloused fingertips, and listened closely to her secret as he made the magic of Brahms come to life on a practically genuine Stradivarius. Of course, later that evening, a revelation fast befell him that in fact he fancied redheads. And so, before the night's end, a crimson-haired barmaid with a chest half-way to Norway was telling anyone who would listen about a little old Dutch couple—grocers—who were sharing shelter and food with those in need.

Perhaps it shouldn't have been surprising that the grocers wouldn't open their door. At the height of the war, visits from strangers always managed to bring trouble. But still, it made no sense. No merchant in these parts would dream of shutting down with the Gestapo around the bend. By now they knew: sell what you have, quickly, before the Germans take it. But what could have happened? Had they been caught? Had they fled without warning? Or did they live in the same bubble as the rest of Albi? She dared not knock a peep louder, but still she had to know.

Quietly, she crept around the alley and peeked her head through the service entrance. The place looked abandoned like a ghost town left in the midst of its daily business. Fresh fruit lined the grocery shelves; an old tin fan struggled to blow heat toward the open room in back. *Au Revoir les Enfants* buzzed with static on a Philco tube radio. In the narrow space behind the counter, a shadowy figure lay sprawled across a checkered marble floor. Slowly, she slid past the stockroom to get a better look. She could finally make out the form on the floor beside the strongbox. The old shopkeeper and his wife had been overcome by a gas leak and were near death when Lea aired out the building and called an ambulance.

In gratitude, the grocers promised her free groceries for life. As though this were no unusual thing, she thought, *Good, now I don't need to worry about money for food.* She was really beginning to like this little town. Hey, what's not to like about free food?

MARY HAD A LITTLE LAMB CHOP

Let's just come out and say it—we Jews have this unnatural fixation with food. A holiday rolls in and it's—"Come on over, we got herring!" A baby boy is born—we snip his schmeckel and bring a platter. Someone dies—cover the mirrors, kiss the widow, and tell her, "I'm so sorry for your loss, honey. We're gonna miss him terrible. Here's a whitefish. It's fresh from Arnie and Richie's." It's a cultural quirk that's sometimes lost on people who've never been hungry. Bubbie was always hungry. So, maybe that's why, for her, food seems to be the answer to absolutely everything.

I remember that my cousin Linda once left Bubbie to watch her newborn for a bit, while she ran to the market. The instruction was simple. "Don't feed him. He's got a sensitive stomach. No food—just the bottle. Okay, Grandma?"

"Right, just the baba. Go on, ve'll be okay. I stay mit my little lamb chop." Well, an hour later Cousin Linda is back, and her baby is covered in vomit. Head to toe he's soaked himself. Naturally, the young mother, in a fury, scours and sniffs the bib looking for any evidence of mischief. And after she uncovers tiny bits of fruit on the baby's hands...

Linda:
(shouting) *Grandma, what the hell did you feed him?*

Bubbie:
Nothing. Nothing. I didn't feed him nothing.

Linda:
What do you mean nothing? Do you see this?

Bubbie stares sheepishly as Linda shakes a puke-stained blanket in frustration.

Linda:

Do you see what this is?

Bubbie is unbending.

Bubbie:

Ya, it looks like vomit.

Linda:

And how'd the vomit get pieces of banana in it?

Bubbie:

I don't know nothing about that.

Linda:

*What do you mean you don't know nothing? Look
at this!*

Bubbie:

*All right, all right. I confess, I confess. But it's
vasn't mine fault. I vas just eating a bissel of
banana, and he kept reaching out to me, reaching
out mit his hungry eyes.*

Linda:

*Grandma, he's five weeks old! He's not reaching for
anything.*

Bubbie:

*He's a growing boy. Trust me, for food like this, he
reaches.*

*Today she's back at it again—standing at the stove, arranging a
little something for our guests. A small crowd has gathered in
the kitchen. Let's Make a Deal was blasting in the den, and no
one wants to listen to a screaming Texan in a cow suit, so they've
settled in the kitchen, watching Bubbie arrange the platter she*

brought from Kosher Kitchen. On the other end of the island are
Cousin Linda and my sister—born-again flower children and veg-
etarians to the bone—just back from an animal rights march
downtown. They're fishing through the fridge for something
vegan, and Bubbie offers her own form of help.

Bubbie:

Dahling, vhat are you looking for?

Linda:

Some salad or veggies. Something with no animal
products.

Bubbie:

Ach, you two are so skinny. You need real food. Try
this. I got it from the market.

Linda:

What's in it?

Bubbie:

It's good. Try it.

Linda:

Uh huh, Grandma, and what's in it?

Bubbie:

Rice, spice, vegetables...it's good.

Linda:

No meat?

Bubbie:

No meat.

Linda:

Are you sure?

Bubbie:

Try it. It's veterinarian.

Linda:

You mean vegetarian?

Bubbie:

Ya, vhatever you vant to call it. It's good. Here...
just a bissel...a tiny bit.

The girls share in their kosher delicacy, licking their chops with
delight as if they'd discovered food for the first time.

Linda:

Wow! This is delicious! What's it called?

Bubbie:

Really, you like it?

Linda:

It's phenomenal. What is it?

Bubbie beams and puffs like a peacock, throwing her chest to the
sky in a show of triumph. Her joy is uncontainable—a sure sign
of trouble.

Linda:

Grandma...what did you do? What's in this?

Bubbie:

Nothing.

Linda:

Grandma!

Bubbie:

Vhat? It's just rice and vegetables...maybe a little
lamb.

In a flash, the vegans turn crimson and burst into convulsions as they dash madly for the sink in a synchronized vomit. Bubbie glows with an indescribable aura of accomplishment.

Bubbie:
See, vhat did I tell you? I knew you'd like it if you tried it.

Sometimes I think you might as well be speaking Mandarin Chinese with a Shanghai accent to her when it comes to things like moral objections to food. I guess for the hungry, every scrap is life. And life—life is a gift to be savored.

CHAPTER XI
HUNGER

....

F ood, then shelter—that was generally the order of things. Seeing
that they had already been blessed with the good fortune to fall into
groceries, the only thing left to do for now was find a safe place to hide.

By this point, the relief agencies were exhausted, and Lea had
learned from her mistake with the farm that it was a waste of time talking to lowly patrolmen. Go straight to the top—that was how to get
things done.

So she settled on the steps of the commissariat waiting for someone—anyone—up in the food chain who could help. "The guy giving
orders must know something," she figured. And there at the threshold
of the police station door, she spotted him— a young lieutenant wrapping up his shift. *Surely a big-shot policeman could do better for me than a
farm*, she thought. And, after a long discussion, the lieutenant agreed—
no farms. True to his word, he steered them clear of the agricultural
sector to a small studio above a paint store.

The building was a run-down, pitch-roofed, squat house that reeked
of paint yet hadn't seen a coat of it since the last Great War. The chipped
plaster walls were covered with a smoky haze of gray ash. The pine
floors were rotted and bowed beneath the weight of each step. Inside,
roaches scuttled anxiously about the store's reception counter in a desperate search for food. Behind the desk dozed a fat, bald man who
looked worse than the bugs that kept him company.

The snoozing merchant quickly woke to the ding of the "ring for
service" bell and greeted the visitors with a warm, hacking cough. He
was a foul slob, this paint man, his body stained with the stench of

bourbon, his crooked teeth marked with the yellow residue of cigarettes that he smoked feverishly to ease the discomfort of his emphysema.

The shopkeeper raised a heavy hand toward an outside staircase and mumbled something about six francs a week. A swig or two later he was face down on the counter again, leaving his lanky brother to lead the way to the upstairs cottage. "Come this way. I'll take you there," a low froggy voice boomed from a scrawny man at the back of the store. The refugees followed warily.

—⁂—

Moving is a simple matter when you've got nothing. They just marched single file up the outside staircase toward their tiny apartment, holding only each other and a few small satchels of clothing and papers. Again, the rotted wood seemed to barely bear the weight of each creaking step.

The squeaky stairway ended at a barren efficiency above the paint storage—one room with just a small kitchen, a table with chairs, and a sunflower-print sofa with a snoring painter face-down on top. He was greasy and pocked with acne scars. His ratty white T-shirt was blotched with red and blue paint, and in the dim light of the loft he looked a little like a drunk French flag.

"Hey, wake up, Sleeping Beauty! Let's go, *Tricolore,* move it." There was no response. The shopkeeper kicked the couch, drew breath to his chest, and then threw his hand to his heart, bellowing the anthem at the top of his lungs. *"Allons enfants de la Patrie. Le jour de gloire est arrivé!"*

The painter leaped from his slumber.

"Ach, come on. Let's go, you lazy do-nothing. I need to bring down the ladder." The guide tilted toward his guests. "Don't worry. That's Maurice. He's an asshole, but he won't bother you."

The path now clear, the skinny landlord climbed onto the couch and lowered a hatch from the ceiling. A ladder stowed snugly inside the garret plummeted to the pine floor. "Your room is up here. You can come down for what you need. This one will either be drunk in here or drunk out there. He won't make any trouble."

Home was literally a hidden attic—one room, no table, no chairs, a small fireplace in the corner, and a bucket for a bathroom. A battered mattress lay dead center on the floor of the room. Too tired to dwell on their squalor, they just dropped to the ground, exhausted, and slept.

—⁓—

It must have been about midnight. First, a subtle pinch below the calf, and then soon blood trickled down their legs and across their fingertips. Like startled sheep, they jumped in unison and then clawed at their flesh, scratching from head to foot. Tiny fleas had picked at them so ravenously that their bodies looked as if they had been cut by a hundred little knives. Try as they might, they couldn't make it stop.

"Quick, throw your clothes into the furnace," Lea ordered as they pitched the little they had left in this world—the clothes on their backs—into the smoldering flames. Watching the crackling fire, she thought about how she wished that bug-ridden apartment would burn just like the insects nesting in their sheets. That night, she prayed for a fire. It was an awful thing to wish for, but she couldn't stop dreaming of that place ablaze—just wishing she could open her eyes and wake up back in the world she'd nearly forgotten.

For hours they scrubbed—trying to scour away any last trace of the vermin that had feasted on them. At sunrise, she returned to the bigshot policeman to see about changing apartments.

"You've got a perfectly good apartment," he told her. "We can't give you another one."

"You call a house full of fleas a good apartment?" she blasted.

"Miss, I think the fleas have more cause to complain than you do."

Lea ranted and hollered and demanded to speak with the commandant. But it was no use. The answer was the same. "Go home, lady. It sounds like you got them all."

Seething with frustration, she raced home to fetch the few scraps of flea-infested linen that had been spared the flames the night before. She was determined to show that big-shot policeman just how bad it was. *Are we all invisible? Does anyone realize what is happening to us?* she wondered. But the husband was hungry, the children were tired, and war—well, war would have to wait until morning.

Battling the world is a tiring business, a heavy strain that only fuels a constant hunger. Oh, G-d, the hunger! What she wouldn't give for a bowl of chicken soup with dumplings. But the only thing more scarce than food was money. And then it hit her—the grocer's promise.

New Holland Market was paradise. Endless rows of the simple things they had almost forgotten were all at their fingertips. For the first time in ages, there was finally enough to burn a proper meal: broth and carrots for soup, red potatoes, even a whole chicken.

Exhausted, Lea set a kettle to boil and sank to the floor. Just a few minutes off her feet—that was all she needed. She had almost settled when she noticed smoke drifting through the apartment. Now, this was nothing unusual. See, like I said, she burned just about everything she cooked. But this time it was coming through the floorboards from the shop below. It turned out that lazy slob from the paint store was having trouble sleeping again—on account of his emphysema. *A smoke'll do the trick*, he figured. And it did. He fell right asleep—with the cigarette still burning in his mouth. Moments later, the whole paint shop was ablaze.

Lea scurried to bring the family down from the ceiling and out of the building. One by one they raced from the attic to the studio and then to the staircase, but fire had already consumed the exit. Cindering pieces of rotted pine trickled to the ground. Jacob and Eva raced down the burning stairs just before it collapsed. But for Lea and Fanny there was no other way but to jump. So they closed their eyes, took a deep breath, and made a leap of faith. There were some bumps, some burns, some bruises, a few broken toes—another blessing from the angels.

—⚌—

May 23, 1941

My dearest Evelyn,

    Things were horrible for a while after the fire. We had no place to go, and nothing to eat after the grocers left town. A day, sometimes two, we'd have no food. But things are better now. We have work and what to eat, and the girls are even in school. The HIAS helped us find a little bungalow, and I got Jacob a job fitting suits in a tailor shop. (You know how this husband won't do nothing for himself.) I help a little, too, sewing uniforms and rolling bandages for the Red Cross. I don't know what happened, but things are better now. It's so quiet—like a dream. I don't know if these people are living in darkness, or I'm finally seeing the light. Everyone is so calm. People talk about the war here, but it's something so faraway, on the other side of the country. Maybe it really will be over soon. That's what people here are saying. They're sure of it. Me, I'm not so sure. But, anyway, for now we are all well. It almost feels like the old days in Belgium again. I like it. Maybe after the war we'll stay here. But I shouldn't get my hopes up, because I know in my heart we'll have to leave. We always have to leave. So keep sending me the papers. The immigration people say maybe fifteen more points, and I can get the visa.

All My Love,
Lea

CHAPTER XII
CAMP

·················

"**N**ever, ever, trust a man to do anything." She should have remembered what her mother had told her a thousand times before whenever her father would gamble away the grocery money, and they'd have to walk clear across town and sell vegetables to the gentiles for meat money. But it was just so simple—go to the *ministère*, get a stamp on the visa, come home. Where could this one have  possibly gone wrong? He had done it twice before with hardly a hitch. But this time, he had to talk. This time he had to confess.

They had asked a question for which there was no true answer: Are you a Jew? The right answer was no. He said yes. That afternoon he was in detention. And sadly, for this, there was no plan.

By sundown, Jacob was in *Camp des Milles*, a French internment camp run by the Vichy. Maybe "camp" wasn't quite the right word. It was more like an abandoned brick factory with an endless row of room-size ovens and huge conveyor belts weaving like a mechanical maze through the shop floor. Outside, the whole place was penned by barbed wire with just two openings—one for the guardhouse and one for the old "eight or thirty" trains (capacity "eight horses or thirty men") that hauled bricks and other cargo to and from the factory.

These days, des Milles had become storage—a warehouse for France's "enemy aliens" (mostly outcast Germans who needed to be watched—basically writers, artists, gays, and critics of the Nazi regime who had managed to make it out alive). But since the occupation, a new wave of "undesirables" had become snarled in the great German extermination net: Jews, Gypsies, mental patients, and a few sad souls who had just pissed off the wrong neighbor. And then there were the partisans— French Resistance, —some communists, some socialists, and a handful of troublemakers who just liked to blow stuff up.

This was the crazy, captive world of Vichy internment. And all of it was miraculously kept safe for the time being through an elaborate and masterful scheme of French disorganization. Nobody knew anything. Everything was lost. Even the most effortless task was somebody else's job.

It was all rather simple in a sense. Chaos bred obscurity; obscurity nurtured survival. So for the moment, everyone waited safely, praying to stay lost in the shuffle.

Don't get me wrong. Des Milles was bad, but it was better than the death camps. It was French, so the work was light. There was cabbage soup and day-old baguette twice a day. On Sundays, if they were lucky and the trains were running, a glass of wine and a sliver of meat might even be negotiated. Mostly, though, they just waited, wandering the caged courtyard and debating the intricacies of art, politics, and philosophy. Des Milles was a cultural menagerie trapped behind chicken wire. It was a place where painters of fame and legend scratched murals with sticks on clay. Grand poets unveiled their secrets of verse and rhyme to eager pig farmers. A table of Nobel laureates sat waiting fruitlessly for food. In the rear of the factory, a gay German drama troupe had even managed to turn a soot covered brick oven into a rather tastefully decorated drag theater called "Die Katakomb," in tribute to the colorful cabaret they'd been forced to abandon. It seems *les dechéts de France*, the misfits of France, had at last found…limbo!

So much of the nation was a state of wait—nervous, unsure— without direction or destination. Men were detained on the streets for questioning; women and children were inventoried and catalogued. "It's just a formality," *le subpréfecture* said, "just for future reference and identification. Nothing to be concerned with." But the part of Europe at that end of the rifle had cause for concern.

Still, registration gave you a number, and a number gave you a roof. For most, that roof rested a few miles north of Des Milles, at an abandoned farmhouse just past the lavender fields, deep in the backcountry of Provence. Conditions were squalid—eighteenth-century rubble of stone and timber that looked untouched since the days of the last French queen. But this Provence—the Provence that hardly knew the sound of belching green army trucks—in all its squalor was still magic. It was an endless lilac horizon with the sound of crickets ringing through the air and the smell of chestnut groves still unblemished by the shelling of tank fire. But in Vichy France, beauty never meant much. Nothing that Hitler touched ever stayed beautiful. Nowhere that Nazi fingers reached could ever be home.

So, they did what they could to make things as they almost remembered them. Sometimes, when the coast was clear, Fanny would slip away to see her father—walking miles alone and sneaking on buses to smuggle him food through the barbed-wire fence. Someone had to fatten him up. Actually, he looked good. He'd put on a bit of weight and had even become popular among the prisoners by making them clothes from old blankets. For the first time ever, you could say he looked a bit round. He said he consumed what he could to stay strong for the work they made him do, but they all knew it was because he preferred the labor camp food to Lea's.

"I don't know what kind of work camp this was," Lea wondered. "What work? They just stood around and talked all day. This he did just fine without soldiers pointing guns on him."

There was no saying when or how, but something about Jacob was different now. He had an inner strength and sense of purpose. She says it was because he finally ate something. He says he had been liberated by the camp.

A LITTLE CONCENTRATION
GOES A LONG WAY

Lately we've been having a hard time figuring out what to do with Bubbie. Despite our best efforts, she just won't get across her head that she's not still the tough, independent go-getter she used to be. Two strokes and three heart attacks later, she still carries on like some crazed fifty-year-old. She keeps her own little condo across the causeway, buses downtown to Bayside, hustles cards on Tuesdays. And it all frightens the hell out of us. We get reports from relatives who say they saw her pushing a shopping cart along the roadway in that not-so-good part of town where she still insists on living. They'd pull up alongside, roll down their windows, and shout, "Lea, what are you doing?" and she'd answer smugly...

Bubbie:
Vat's it look like I'm doing? I'm going shopping at Lorenzo's.

Cousin Phil:
But Lorenzo's is like a mile away.

Bubbie:
Ya, I know vhere it is. You vant I should bring you back someting?

But, as hard as it is to accept, the not-so-simple truth is that she needs the unthinkable—she needs help. She loses count of her medications, she struggles with stairs. And forget about her see-ing any doctor besides the sainted Dr. Silverman ("He's a good Jewish boy—the only doctor who listens to vat I'm saying"), which I guess would be fine, except he's an optometrist, and she's got heart trouble.

We really figured one of these assisted living facilities would be the answer. Places with names like "Pleasant Acres" and "Sunshine Ranches"—names that make no sense at all to an old Jew from Lodz.

Bubbie:

Vhat, I'm a horse? Vhat I'm gonna do on a sunny ranch? But, if you really vant I should try it...

Somehow, we thought it was best. Or maybe we just thought it would work. So, my aunt pulled every string she could and got her into some of Miami's finest homes. Of course, in a record-setting span of five months, she managed to get herself thrown out of every single one of them—six different facilities in five months. They called her unmanageable. "It's a concentration camp," she'd shout, pounding her lunch tray on the table. "They're concentrating people. Can you believe it? All day long these people vait around to die—like a death camp. In Europe I ran to get out from the concentration camps, and after all that, you gonna put me there now? I'll escape. I escaped from Hitler, I can escape from here."

Now she's on a list, and we're all in a pickle. We know she can't be on her own, but nobody will take her. Cousin Linda was brave enough to try, and so for a while, Bubbie lived in Linda's guest cottage. But then Bubbie started breaking out and disappearing for hours on end. One day my cousin was having a casual conversation with her over tea. Linda went to heat some more water and when she came back, Bubbie had vanished. After a day of our frantic calls to every police department and emergency room in town, Bubbie shows up at the door just before dusk with a red-flowered Carmen Miranda dress flung over her shoulder. Of course, my cousin, in a frenzy, asks her...

Cousin Linda:

Grandma, where the hell have you been? You've had everyone worried sick about you.

Bubbie:

I vent to Sears.

Cousin Linda:

Sears? What the hell were you doing at Sears?

Bubbie:

Vhat, I can't go to the mall to get a dress for my grandson's vedding?

Cousin Linda:

Grandma. That's crazy.

Bubbie:

Vhy? Vat's the vorst ting that could happen to me?
I die? They kill me? I'm old. I'm supposed to die.
You need to vorry if I'm afraid to die.

Bubbie has this gift for saying things for which there are no answers. So for now, life's exactly the way she wants it—with her in control. She's back in her apartment, pushing her wobbly little shopping cart wherever she damned well pleases. After all, none of us have escaped from hell and lived to bring three children, seven grandchildren, and twelve great-grandchildren into the world on our own. What do we know?

CHAPTER XIII
LA COTE D'AZUR

···

By February 1941, France was in shambles. Europe was in chaos. The world was at war. At the consul's office, the gossips were telling crazy stories about the occupation creeping farther south through Provence. Lea took those rumors seriously. Too many times they'd proved true.

She raced home and gathered what bundles she could carry. Just the essentials: a few scraps of clothing, whatever money was in the room, and of course, her priceless US immigration affidavits. To her, these were gold—their ticket to America. She clutched the precious papers tightly as she rounded up the children. The girls knew the drill. This wasn't the first time they had fled their home in the middle of the night. Within minutes they were out the door and headed to the train station—their lives flung haphazardly into the canvas satchels strewn across their shoulders.

There was enough money to get to the Mediterranean, so that's where they went. They settled just north of the Cote D'Azur—outside the port city, Marseille. The province was under Vichy control, but for now seemed relatively safe. The Vichy were rabid anti-Semites, but better than the Nazis.

—⟋⟍—

Soon, Provence had no Jews. That's maybe the easiest thing to remember. By March, the trucks had taken most of them. You could feel the wave that had rushed through the seashore; taste the scent that something terrible had changed this place forever. There was only quiet and the aftermath—like the leaves that linger and dust that drifts through the air after a frightful storm. A cold silence spoke of what had happened: gunshots echoing from building to building; doors kicked down in the middle of the night; screaming children ripped from their mother's arms; an old woman begging to take her cat. Behind closed curtains and locked doors, the pale eye of a curious neighbor peered through a peephole, weeping with pity and then thanking all creation it wasn't him or his.

It wasn't even a month since they'd left their last hovel, and this hovel was getting bad. Refugees from as far south as Toulon were saying there was no place left to go. Not in France anyway. "Head to Spain," the rumor mill squeaked. "Franco's got too many problems to worry about Jews."

But these days, everybody had a theory, and everybody was wrong.

"The Swiss will take you if you pay them ten thousand Francs."

"The Russians will let you in if you say you're a communist and sign up to fight in Siberia."

In the end, who really knew anything? Except to run and keep running.

The ministry was saying St. Michel. It was small. It was quiet. It was unimportant enough for the Germans not to bother for a while. By Thursday, it was home. As for Jacob, well…I guess for now, the husband would have to wait.

CHAPTER XIV
ESCAPE

·····················

What made her do it, who could say? But some compelling force—
less than love, more than the rote duties of family—drove her
back to des Milles— back to Jacob—back to the good tailor she called
her husband. No matter what, it would never happen to them. Her children would never be fatherless and hungry. Her children would never
be like her.

So she set out for Aix-en-Provence, past the lavender fields, across
the old Italian trade routes far north to the ominous Camp des Milles.
Two trains and a coal-powered bus later, she had reached the banks of
the River Rhone.

The old brick factory stood alone in the countryside—cordoned by
barbed wire and makeshift trenches. Cold and industrial, the building
was a great square warehouse with a network of catwalks and pulleys
hanging high above the shop floor. Scrawled about the unfinished brick
walls, random murals in rainbow colors painted pictures of camp life
and the rich rewards of hard labor. At the fringe of the compound, a
barbed wire wall wove and climbed five meters high, wrapping the place
on all sides.

That day, like most things French, was hazy. A coal-colored sky
was peppered thick with clouds eager to gush rain. At the gatehouse, a
young *milicien Français* stood watch alone while his commander waited in the administration office screaming at the soccer semifinals that
crackled on a crickety RCA Victor. Quietly—meekly—she bade him
bon jour and presented her papers for entry, as she'd done a dozen times

before. She smiled warmly, signed her name as always, and walked arrow straight to a receiving station.

At first it was the usual—families all around sharing pictures of troubled children and weeping about the war. "Keep him steady. Keep him focused," she reminded herself over and again.

"Jacob, do you want to get out of here?" she whispered, her lips pressed close to his ear. Jacob stared blankly. "Jacob, do you want to leave?" she repeated, only to meet more confusion. "Jacob, listen to what I am saying. We are going to escape." Suddenly reality began to register, and Jacob's color fast fled. He started to panic. "Lea, no…Don't…We can't…"

"Stay calm, Jacob," she whispered, "and follow my lead."

Jacob knew there wasn't a choice. The decision was done.

He followed warily to the gatehouse where the young sentinel was still busy, waiting patiently for nothing. As if on cue, Lea threw her hands to her stomach and fell to the floor beside the guard's feet.

Jacob fast found courage from parts unknown. "My wife, she has a condition. She needs her medication. Please, we can help her, but she needs to get to a doctor." And then the rain began to pour with a fury even spring never saw.

The guard gazed at the long walk across the muddy courtyard and then toward his commander, who was still busy cursing the mothers of half the southern soccer conference.

Jacob was fast on his feet. "Look, I'll take her to the bus stop. It's just around the bend. I'll be back in two shakes."

The guard glanced again at Lea and then at his boss, who was still leaned back with his belly in the air, relishing the privileges of rank.

"Please," Lea begged, "where's he gonna go?" The soldier pondered, peeked once more, and then waved a rifle toward the gate. "*Allez*—go," he whispered. "Here, take an exit pass in case they stop you."

Once clear of the gate, they ducked behind a wall and never came back. She just decided—to hell with the Germans and the French, "that husband is coming home to take care on his family."

SOME THINGS ARE
WORTH FIGHTING FOR

Burned cheese blintzes and cheap instant coffee—you can smell it a mile away. Most of the crowd has congregated in the living room to listen to Leon play his usual repertoire of songs. Bubbie has joined my Grandma Anna and Aunt Pauline on the couch to debate the finer points of bunion removal. Grandma Anna is my mother's mother. She's kind of a true-life version of Edith Bunker from All in the Family.

Anna:
Oh, Pauline, I don't undastand why you gotta say
such awful tings.

Pauline:
Oh, Anna, go fuck yourself.

That's Aunt Pauline, my grandma Anna's sister. She'll probably require some explaining. Actually, she'll probably require a lot of explaining. Aunt Pauline is a woman who gives new meaning to the phrase "tough as nails." She's seventy-six years old and barely five feet tall, but she can bring a rosy blush to a roomful of drunken sailors. She has this gift for extreme candor.

Pauline:
You better move, I just farted.

My uncle, Stanley, joins the discussion. He's a charmer, which gets a person absolutely nowhere with Pauline.

Stanley:
Pauline, you look wonderful. I love what you did
with your hair.

She puts her arm around him warmly,

Pauline:

Stanley, go fuck yourself.

Stanley:

*(He bends to kiss her cheek.) You know, Pauline,
I'd been here over an hour without you saying
something nasty to me. I was beginning to worry
that something was wrong. Well, I'll see you later,
Beautiful. I've got to go check how my mother's
doing in the other room with Sara.*

Stanley's mother is Toby. The ravages of age have made Toby progressively more deaf and senile, which has actually made her a lot more interesting than when she had it together. She'll sit at the piano and play songs, but not realizing what she's playing, at the exact same time she'll sing a completely different song in a completely different key and tempo. It's an incredible sight! As usual, they've got her at a table with my aunt Sara. Sara is a sweet old blind woman. The two of them talk for hours. One can't see, and the other can't hear, but somehow they manage to engage in stimulating conversations—rarely at the same time and never about the same topic, but they seem to enjoy each other's company. Sara knows that Toby doesn't understand what she's saying, but she chats with her anyway. Toby laughs a lot lately, and it's nice to hear people laugh.

Right now, everyone is just waiting to eat. The food has been delayed for a while until my uncle Erwin can get there. He's the only one who can read enough Hebrew to do the blessings.

To pass time until the cooking is ready, the grandmothers have moved to the den. They're watching a household favorite TV show—Family Feud. This episode features Joe Black and his family taking on the White family from Detroit. To further complicate matters, the Blacks are white and the Whites are black.

The bluehairs call a play-by-play that sounds like something out of a bad "Who's on First" skit.

Pauline:

Hey, Anna, you think the colored family'll win?

Anna:

Who, the Whites?

Pauline:

No, the colored family.

Anna:

That's what I said—the Whites.

Pauline:

Does that family look white to you?

Anna:

No, their name is White.

Pauline:

A colored family named White? Then who the hell are the other people?

Anna:

The Blacks.

Pauline:

Oh, go fuck yourself, Anna.

They wrestle to pick up the pieces of a black-and-white world turned upside down.

Anna:

Would you listen for a minute, Pauline? The colored family is named White, and the white family is named Black.

Pauline:

Oh, for cryin' out loud, Anna. Why do I even bother talkin' to you? I swear, next you'll be tellin' me some cock 'n' bull story about Chinamen named Goldberg.

Bickering is a favorite pastime of the sisters. They studied the art with a master back in the old country—Brooklyn. Bubbie remains unusually quiet. She's learned from experience it's best to stay out of fights that aren't her own.

CHAPTER XV

THE BATTLES OF A BOURGEOIS MARXIST

··

March 1941. Jacob is back. He's a communist now. Just like that—he's a communist. Lea wondered, "All of a sudden a communist? What, they don't make you take a class, a test, nothing?" Jacob had been speaking with the men in the camp, who explained how one day society would have no bigotry, no religions, no division among classes.

It all made perfect sense. Bigotry seemed a good thing to lose. He could live without religion for as long as his banned him from pork chops and bacon. And a classless society—who wouldn't want that? Lea was stunned by the stupidity. "A bourgeois communist? What kind of businessman becomes a communist? You wanted a change, you couldn't become a welder or a shoemaker or something? How you gonna make a living as a communist?"

Her advice whisked through one ear and out the other. These days Jacob was different—passionate and determined. He ranted endlessly about joining his "comrades in the struggle against the Fascist regime." He prophesized of "the grand revolution" and the "rise of the secretariat," the "prochariot"—or something like that.

None of it made sense to Lea. "What kind of revolution is a tailor going to make? A coat, he can make. Pants, I seen him make. A revolution—this I don't know from."

But Jacob had made up his mind. It was his chance to be more than a simple tailor. And if he couldn't be more than just a tailor, at least he'd be free of his wife's henpecking for a while.

So he joined the French underground—a group whose name even confused Lea. They called it the underground—so you'd figure a bunch of guys crawling around and hiding in smelly sewers all day. But they didn't go underground. They met at Saul Fischer's house or in the English Pub, which, mind you, stank just fine, too.

Make no mistake, it wasn't easy for Jacob to muster the courage to join the Resistance. The man had an inherent fear of—well, of everything. But the fact of the matter was he had two choices: go and fight the Nazis or stay and fight his wife. Jacob decided to take his chances with the Germans.

The partisans racked their brains to find some use for a 110-pound tailor. The only safe thing was to keep him clear of combat—assembling equipment, counting ammunition, that sort of thing. He was swift and clever. And soon his skillful hand and endearing spirit earned him a promotion to captain of the Resistance Bartending Squad. He called it field operations and said he was off to battle the "Fascist invaders." As quickly as he had settled, Jacob was gone.

He'd take off for days, sometimes weeks, at a time. Bordeaux, Tours, Lyon—Lea never knew where he was headed. He'd go to meet Saul at the pub or at some top-secret checkpoint, disappear for a while, and then show up in the middle of the night, shushing Lea so she wouldn't wake the kids.

By the end of April, he claimed to be blowing up bridges somewhere in Lyon. He wasn't expected to be gone long. But to Lea the trip seemed an eternity, because she had big news to tell him: they were having another child.

CHAPTER XVI
SOMEBODY

∙∙∙∙∙∙∙∙∙∙∙∙∙∙∙∙∙∙∙∙∙∙∙∙∙∙∙∙∙

Everyone knew those damned poles never seemed to bring good news. You've probably seen them—those huge candy-striped pillars in the middle of town where they post orders of assistant deputy ministers and Citroens for sale. This time, though, was different. It was the kind of message that made you gasp—the sort of terror that could start you pacing like a caged animal looking for a break in the bars. They said it was a mandate from Petain himself. "In the spirit of collaboration toward peace and by decree of the *Etat Francais*, a census is hereby ordered to be conducted throughout southern France. Present to the *subpréfecture* by September 30. Cooperation is obligatory."

And so, by the start of October 1941, things had become complicated, and Jacob's back was to the wall—in every imaginable sense. Fighting was futile. Leaving, impossible. Soldiers scoured every corner, checking papers, counting heads. There was nothing to do but wait and weep for dear France. Patrols were at all ends. So, the five-man resistance cell did what little they could—they hid. Gypsies living in the basement of Lea's apartment opened up their home to them and then sealed it from behind—a fake brick wall to hide behind until things got better. But Jacob knew this couldn't go on for long. He needed to do something for France. He needed to get out. He needed papers.

The death of Jean-Claude Cazeau was a most peculiar and fortuitous event. Jacob had met Jean-Claude's cousin—Jean-Marc, the welder—at Camp Des Milles when the Germans issued a requisition for metal-workers to build impregnable gates and a new barbed wire perimeter around the camp.

"Why" was a question they never answered, nor was it a question that those in the habit of breathing ever ventured to ask. Jean-Marc was there to do a job, and he did it. But when he wasn't doing that job, the welder and the tailor got to talking. Well, one thing led to another, and then another, and eventually to the unfortunate story of ill-fated Cousin Claude, as folks called him.

Cousin Claude was a likable enough guy, a life-of-the-party sort, but he had always been the black sheep of the Cazeau family—employed by no one and indebted to everyone, still searching for his calling, so long as the hours were light, and pay was stellar. That is, until he saw that poster in the bakery window: SEE THE WORLD. SAVE. SERVE. DEFEND. JOIN THE FOREIGN LEGION.

He had images of oil money coming out of his ears and of harems of beautiful belly dancers fanning his forehead and feeding him figs. So he signed himself up for a tour in the Sahara, and something in him changed. He became a man. He even earned himself a couple of medals in Tangiers—surviving three air raids and rescuing the niece of a Dutch diplomat—only to end up dead in a freak camel accident. They said it hardly ever happened to anyone. And so, for the modest price of forty francs and a finely cut coat, Jacob found himself a Frenchman— Legionnaire with Distinction—Jean-Claude Cazeau. Jacob had his papers. Jacob was somebody.

But by early November, there was no avoiding the decision that had to be made. Searches were now commonplace, deportations the daily norm. Neighbors sent neighbors to the death trains for bars of soap and boxes of chocolates. Everyone was to be accounted for, and the whole south of France was peering through closed curtains and counting. Slowly, with each report of more Nazis patrolling the vacant rues of Vichy, the executioner's noose was inching tighter and tighter. Even documented *Francais* were being detained. And on the streets, a lone pregnant woman with two children was hardly cause for concern—just a woman shopping for the day's necessities: warm milk, yesterday's fresh baguette. But a whole family together in the middle of the day? There was no hiding it. They were running!

Maybe Saul was right. Maybe it was time for Jacob to take a stand and become the man he was pretending to be. Clearly, this war couldn't be won without loyal partisans laying their lives and families on the line to fight for the brotherhood and the cause. And it sure as hell couldn't be won without someone to pour their drinks and toast victory at the end of it all.

So, for now, it was settled, Jacob was charging off with the Resistance. He said his comrades needed him. Lea decided. "They can keep him."

GOING ONCE, GOING TWICE...GONE

Bubbie has been through a husband or two, or maybe three. She's always just found herself going in a different direction than the rest of the world, or maybe the rest of the world just could never keep up.

Husband number one, you've met—the meek tailor with the heart of gold. Husband number two (well, sort of husband number two—the jury is still out on whether there was really ever a wedding) was a kind and gentle Manhattan slumlord with buckets of money. He came from Russia scratching and clawing for every penny he ever made. And the truth is, not a day went by that he didn't shower all he had on my grandmother. They were a picture of old-world order and stability. And really, life was quite settled for them on the Upper West Side. At last, the future looked secure. Hell, she might have stayed forever, basking in good fortune, had her kids not packed up and gone to Florida.

So one November day, she and Sam, his name was, were talking dreams the way married folks do when the weather's bitter cold, and the coffee's warm to the bone, and she complained how the ice was unbearable, and someday she'd like to be closer to her kids in Florida. Well, for her, "someday" meant tomorrow, and for him it meant maybe every other winter. And so, when he finally grumbled in that thick Siberian accent, "Bah, why you want to go down there for? You got everything you need here," she just packed up and left the next day without so much as a note. She figured if he really knew her, he'd understand. That's always been her way.

She says she must have been a Gypsy in another life, but I think that when you've been through hell for your kids, managing without them isn't just hard—it's impossible. I guess Sam never got that and ended up left in the cold.

CHAPTER XVII
VISIONS

·····················

Sunrise. December 28, 1941. It was time. The baby was coming, and Lea needed to find somewhere to deliver. A hospital was out of the question—they'd ask for paperwork, which could only lead to problems. She didn't know any midwives, and she certainly wasn't about to have her child in the bushes like the Indians her father had told her about. Besides, even in the south, the winter cold was unbearable this time of year. So, she settled on the home for unwed mothers. They wouldn't ask too many questions there. "Those girls" don't usually like to talk about their predicaments.

They muddled through the narrow, windy streets of *Le Panier*, down an ancient alleyway with arched gateways to an old, brick building on a busy cobblestone thoroughfare. A large but flimsy sign swung westward in the wind: SAINT MICHEL'S HOME FOR UNWED MOTHERS. In those days, the Church was hardly discreet and accommodating when it came to sinners. Welcome or not, it looked warm, so they raced through the doorway, blew heat to their hands, and settled in a crowded vestibule. An ancient woman with loose dentures hunched heavily over the reception counter. She coughed and criticized with the same breath.

"Next! Let's go! We haven't got all day. Fill this out—and don't skip anything." The old woman hacked as she shoved a small stack of forms in the young mother's direction. Lea quickly complied—except for the part about the child's father. Too much information would surely make trouble. She handed the half-answered inquiry to the receptionist, who shoved it right back. "Psst. Psst. Come now, girl. Confession is the path to salvation. Go on. Tell us everything. Spare no filthy detail."

She could feel the shame of these husbandless women, as she told the gray-haired clerk her story—or at least, the first one that came to mind. She said that the child's father was a French airman whom she barely knew and that he had abandoned her to go bomb Italians in Africa.

The old woman leered, rolling her eyes from Lea's swollen belly to the two girls at her hip. She could stand no more. "You breed like rabbits, you Spanish. Didn't you learn from your first two mistakes? Never mind, just come with me." Lea wanted so badly to correct this loud-mouthed old fossil, and explain how her husband was fighting to save France with Saul Fischer over at the English Pub, but her pride would get them all killed. So she just bit her lip and followed the toothless woman.

The receptionist led her to a kindly midwife named Marie. Marie promised that, for now, the girls would be safe with the sisters from Saint Michel's. She knew it would be better for them there. Lea was in no shape to care for her children, and the German soldiers always seemed to steer clear of churches when they were winning.

By the chime of the morning church bell, the nuns were at the doorstep. Lea squeezed her girls and followed Marie to a makeshift maternity ward where worried women lumbered in waiting.

Troubled and tired, she settled beside a haggard Hungarian who ranted tirelessly of a husband who was soon to come. "He'll rescue me," the blue-eyed stranger cried. "My Stephan—he'll come for me." The Germans had taken him away, and everybody knew *you don't come back from the places they take you*. But she insisted he would return.

A young nun naïvely tried to make her see reason. "Dear, he's surely in G-d's merciful hands now," she gently whispered. The Hungarian turned red with rage and to spite the sister bit her own lip until it bled. For hours, she refused to speak. She wouldn't permit that nun to steal her last sliver of hope with a comforting smile. Battered, bloody, and spiteful, she wallowed patiently in her bitterness—moaning and grunting, but speaking to no one. And then he was born, and soon, at last, the words returned. Cradling her screaming infant, she cried to heaven,

"Stephan, your boy. Your beautiful baby boy! Oy, can you see him, sweetie? Ooohh!" Her lips puckered tightly as she kissed his glimmering head. "He's a baldie—just like his father!" They took the child, and she wept bitter tears through the night.

—◆—

Maybe it was the stress. Maybe it was just time. But Lea fell into labor moments later and continued for nearly twelve hours. She flailed and screamed as white-gowned matrons wrung their hands and prayed for no more complications. The strain of the war and the running had taken a heavy toll on her body, making it a struggle for her to function, let alone deliver a child. Like the rest of Europe, she had succumbed to that perpetual sickness that fell like a heavy fog over the entire continent. Her temperature soared. At times she'd flutter in and out of consciousness. Other times she'd hallucinate.

She imagined dead relatives gathered around her—real old-time Jewish bubbies and zeydas—grandmas and grandpas—with covered heads and long black clothes. Her aunt Sophie was knitting a sweater. Her uncle Meyer, the butcher, was complaining about the heat. "Open the window. It's burning in here," he cried. "Open the window!" Lea parroted the instruction. "Open the window, it's hot." The midwife stood puzzled. "It's freezing outside. I can't open the window." Lea repeated, shouting over and again, "Open the window! Open the window!" They had tried all else to no end, so they did as she asked.

Lea settled quickly. She could hear Uncle Meyer. "Oy, that's better. Not so warm." Her fever slowly dropped, and she began to regain strength. Color crept back into her face, and the hallucinations gradually faded. Later that evening, cooled by the breath of a howling December wind, she gave birth to a baby boy. She named him Max Pierre. Max—for her sweaty uncle Meyer—and Pierre, the French word for stone, because he would need to be strong like a rock for the journey ahead.

A SORROWFUL SEA OF STONE

There's this thing with Jews and rocks that maybe I should explain. For us, the rocks we choose in life are important. When we're young, they entertain us—playful things to skip across Surprise Lake or through the windshield of a '79 Firebird. As we grow, they're the ground beneath our feet and guide us where to go. Finally, in the end, they sit atop our graves and mark that we were here and did something.

They say we leave them to remember. You can see it at the Jewish cemetery. There's hardly a flower to be found—just pebbles and marble everywhere. Flowers fade. Stones are forever. So all around you'll spot restless Jews with noses to the ground, looking for just the right stone to set on the graves of their dearly departed—a humble gesture to show that they haven't forgotten. Sometimes, if you've lived a special life, there are piles of them, a tiny mountain of memory stacked on all sides like dusty gray poker chips. They're simple, earthly tokens that say you mattered to somebody. You never want to be a Jew with no rocks.

These days, though, it's hard to think of rocks and not remember Cousin Ari—Linda's daughter and Bubbie's oldest great-granddaughter. She was seventeen and special—a tiny little honors kid who wore glasses, helped animals, and listened to her mother. It was hard to believe that she could be so sick—Crohn's disease with intestinal cancer—an unwelcome inheritance of a bitter family legacy.

And for as long as we could, we kept it from Bubbie. We had to. She had already lost her own child to that wicked disease. Her poor heart just couldn't handle another. Not at her age. She just wasn't strong enough to take it.

So at all hours of the night—while fighting for their little girl's life—my cousins would quietly sneak past Bubbie's little cottage, coast the car to the street and race with all due speed to the emergency room. "She's at camp, Grandma," or "She's at a Humane Society rally," they'd say—fighting back the tears and pain behind the thin facade of a troubled smile.

When Ari eventually passed (and it was finally time to tell Bubbie), there was a crowd a mile long at the cemetery. Endless rows of animal shelter volunteers and sick kids she'd helped came from all over, donning black funeral wear and Ari's trademark red Converse sneakers—their way to show they remembered. And then later there were stones—like nothing you could imagine—so different from the gray quarry-rock graves of the "Beloved Mothers—Grandmothers—Great-Grandmothers" all around her. From corner to corner, this child's resting place was buried in beauty—smooth, brilliant rocks from every part of the world brought by everyone who'd ever loved her—a rainbow sea of sorrow. There is this thing with Jews and rocks...

CHAPTER XVIII
MARSEILLE

·····························

The rocky shore of Marseille is a sight to behold in the morning's first light. Waves crash on a barren beach. Shrieking seagulls fight for the early worm or whatever it is that they squawk about at six o'clock in the morning. The noises of nature ring clear and constant. Funny that such a ruckus suddenly seemed so peaceful—so normal. It was like an ancient memory of a summer trip to the coast they had taken years ago. All you could see was serene—almost tropical. Salty air whiffed a slight scent of fish. Date palms danced in a lukewarm breeze. Fisherman cursed neighbors and neighbors' mothers over netting rights and prized market spaces. A pastel-colored beach town was seashore business as usual. Nothing here was being blown to shards. Not in Marseille. Not yet.

There was only a sunrise, a blanket, and a baby—that's all. But not much else mattered besides leaving. Don't overstay a welcome or stick around one place too long—Jews had learned that lesson well by now. Keep moving; press forward—somewhere, anywhere, in steady retreat from the cancerous occupation that spread all around them.

They'd been three nights in the safety and shelter of the *maternité*, but now that was done. All that remained was another chirping mouth in a chorus of strife and hunger.

Who knows? Maybe he'd be fine. He was big and beefy and insulated like a seal, but the winter wind could take her bite from even the best of them. So she set out for something, anything, to give him shelter: a basket, a box, some scrap to call a bed.

—⋙—

Garbage these days wasn't what it used to be, but it was someplace to start—a trove of treasures and things discarded. By now the port was abuzz with shippers moving the commodities of war, so surely there'd be more abandoned than the better half of Europe. But the rubbish was gone—ravaged by scavengers done with their day long before the early bird had even lifted a wing. So, empty-handed (well, sort of), she headed for the docks.

The docks of Marseille run lengthwise along the *canaver*—a kilometer-long boardwalk of cargo ships and fishing trawlers sardined into tiny berths along the water view. But don't think Paris or even the riverfront. This was a sketchy place—a region of roughneck sailing men with the tattoos and gunmetal to prove it.

Unafraid or unaware, she approached a freighter moored beside the boardwalk and called to a deckhand high atop the ship's bow. "*Monsieur, un panier, si vous plait?* A basket, please?" she pleaded.

"If you want charity, lady, go to the church. We've got nothing for you here," shouted the shadowy figure at the pulpit.

"Please," she grabbled, "I just need a bed for my baby. Whatever you have. Anything, I beg you."

The shadow shimmered and spoke roughly. "Oh yeah, pick him up. Let me see him."

With a mother's pride, she hoisted her newborn high toward the twilight creeping in above the horizon. "Can you see him?" she cried. "My baby, can you see him?"

The shadow faded and then grumbled gruffly, "Yeah. I see him. He's got a big head, that one—like a melon."

The silhouette soon vanished, and all that remained was the hollow sound of creaking boats and crashing waves rushing against the rocky seawall—the noises of dawn in a sleepy port town. It was the image of a new day breaking as the cackle of contented gulls faded and slowly drifted south with the seaweed. Light, now in full bloom, gently blanketed the shore.

Lea looked again to an awakening sky and wept a prayer. "Please, something? Anything?" she cried for no one to hear.

And when all seemed lost a voice rang out from above. "Here...for Melonhead." From high atop the bow of the ship a wicker fruit basket tumbled to the ground.

With a grateful *merci*, she took her Melonhead and her basket and headed to the steps of Saint Michel's. She found a quiet spot, beat the bugs from the basket, set her baby inside. And then she told the nuns, "I'm here for my children."

CHAPTER XIX
UN BEBÉ FRANÇAIS

···

The ministry could be bribed, but that meant money. Friends were few and far away. Those still lingering straddled the relief line.

At the Red Cross, there were blankets; the JDC had food, sometimes. And shelter—well, shelter was a government dole. And government doles had just one unbending rule: French first.

"Pssst. Pssst. Come on, girls," Lea warned as she wrestled for attention. "Stand up straight, and look French." She struggled to seem normal while feeling like death warmed over. Her muscles ached to the brink of failure. A sea of phlegm still swirled in her chest. Her throat rattled like a clunky icebox.

The girls had their own distractions, too. "Mama, the baby is so cute! Can we play with him?"

"Will he drink a bottle like a little doll?"

"Will he hold my finger?"

"I want to carry him!"

"Why does he cry?"

"What does he eat?"

"I'll explain that later," she answered as she sniffled and sneezed and slithered a small step farther down the relief line. "Now, stay quiet and follow me."

Two hours and twenty pleas of "Mama, may I" later, a voice barked from beyond a sea of swirling heads, "Mothers with small children to the left, everyone else to the right. Come on. Let's go. There's no food today, just forms. If you're not native French, don't bother—we're full. Next!"

For Lea, the sound of the cattle call was already common. She struggled to contain her cough and look like just another healthy troubled face.

"Okay, step forward. Let me see him," the voice called from behind the counter. "How old is he?"

The young mother stared sheepishly at the relief worker now eying her napping newborn. "He's two days," she slowly exhaled in response.

"Okay, does he have any papers?"

Again a blank stare as she fumbled through her bag. The nuns had given her something—a document—stamped and sealed. It said, "Baby Boy. Max Pierre Lazega. Born 12/29/1941, 11:05 p.m., Marseille, France. Mother: Lea Lazega. Father: Unknown." The stamp dropped, a harried signature was scrawled—"Go on, hurry along. This says who you see to get a place to stay."

For today, at least, they were French.

—◊◊◊—

Early evening. The baby was in his basket. The girls were on the floor, complaining again of hunger. A knock at the door was loud and sudden.

"*Qui est-ce?*—Who is it?" she asked warily, knowing that Nazis never knock.

"Hey, does Melonhead eat bananas?" moaned the mysterious voice at the door.

"Bananas?" she answered puzzled by the question.

"Oui, does he eat fruit? You know—Eek! Eek! Ah! Ah!—like Bobo the monkey," the door replied. "Does he like fruit?"

"Why? What are you talking about?"

"I've got something for you—bananas—a box of them down at the dock. Wrong shipment. Boss says we're stuck with them, and they gotta go."

So it was…dinner was served. Bananas in the evening. Bananas in the morning. Bananas until they rotted purple.

114

Melons. Melon-head. Tête de Melon. The name seemed to stick and maybe with reason. I mean, it did kind of fit. His noggin was great and round and blushed red from the cold that nipped at his dimpled cheeks. Everything about him was plump and ripe to squeeze. So maybe it wasn't such a bad thing to be called around here—Melonhead. In this place anything sweet was a blessing.

—⁓—

It was later that evening. She had almost lost the nerve to write since Albi, nearly forgotten that there was a world beyond the one relentlessly collapsing around her. She reached for her handbag and then turned over what was left in it: the scraps and remnants of harried lives tumbled onto the empty dinner table in front of them. "Damn it! I know I had a pen from that consul somewhere in here," she grumbled to herself. But there was just an envelope—unopened and forgotten since Albi. It was a letter from Evelyn with just a short, stinging message. It said that Esther had died from starvation in the ghetto. There was no turning back time. No chance to try again. All that was left was the note on the floor, stained with tears and bitter memories.

A EULOGY TO REMEMBER

No one shines at a funeral like Uncle Stanley. While the others are busy weeping for the return of What's My Line, Uncle Stanley is painstakingly preparing for his oldest customer's funeral tomorrow. At ninety-two years old, Lina Goldfarb has seen her last pin curler, and it's fallen to Uncle Stanley, as usual, to find just the right words to remember her by. As Miami Beach's beautician to the rich and not-so-famous, folks just figure he can do for them in death what he did for them in life—make them look good. This time, though, he's stuck. Reaching for that elusive thought, he paces briskly across the terrazzo and scratches through his lines.

Stanley:
*...and Lina was...Lina was...nasty and impossible.
Boy, am I stuck on this one.*

Anna:
Oh, yeah, I heard this morning that Lina died.

Grandma Anna keeps tabs on everyone who dies before her.

Anna:
*Whadda ya' gonna say, Stanley? "Her husband left
her more money than Rockafella and she never
spent a nickel of it?"*

Stanley:
I don't know. This one's a toughie.

Anna:
*I don't get it. I thought she always gave you a hard
time.*

Stanley:

She did. She gave everybody a hard time. I remember the first time I met her. It was my first day at the salon. I was slammed with a million customers and running like twenty minutes behind. So, I'm a little backed up, and she's my 12:00, and I have no idea she owns half of Miami Beach, so I've got her waiting in the lobby until I can get to her. Anyway, she storms in, right smack in the middle of my 11:30, and says, "You need to finish her now because I'm your 12:00, and I've got a lot to do today." So I tell her, "I'm sorry, lady, but you'll have to wait your turn like everyone else." And she turns red and shouts, "I don't think so! Do you have any idea who I am?" So I put my hand on her shoulder and tell her, "I'm sorry, honey, I don't. But that happens to a lot of people your age. Maybe you should have it tattooed on your arm so you don't keep forgetting." After looking like her head was gonna explode, she finally turns to me and says, "You know what...you're kind of funny. I think I like you." She stayed with me for twenty-six years after that and sent me everyone she knew. Never dropped an appointment or forgot any of my kids' birthdays. Actually, you know what, I really am gonna miss her. Maybe I'll say she was the most driven and committed person I ever met.

This guy really does have a gift.

Bubbie:

Oy, he's good. Hire him now for my funeral.

The change of tune is sudden. Toby's loose, and she's got the piano. She's playing that Barbara Streisand Cats song and crying hysterically as her skinny fingers fumble across the ivories. She *starts to sing something else but can't get past the tears. Her face is droopy, and her voice cracks. And with her long nose and squinty eyes, she kind of looks a little like Mr. Magoo—but better looking.*

Bubbie sees the scene from the couch and reaches to comfort an old friend in distress. Pitter-pattering across the room, she slides beside Toby onto a wobbly piano bench, wriggling herself into place as she rests a gentle hand on Toby's shoulder.

Bubbie:

Toby, Dahling, vhat's the matter?

Toby:

It's awful. Just awful.

The tears pour like bathwater.

Bubbie:

Dahling, vhat's awful?

Toby:

It's terrible. So terrible. I just heard...

That should have been the first clue—Toby never hears anything right, and when she does, she forgets what she heard and comes back with a completely different story.

Toby:

Oh, Lea. Oh, Lea. It's such a tragedy. Just terrible.

Bubbie's patience slices thin like deli meat.

Bubbie:

Toby, enough. Say it already. Vhat's so terrible?

Toby:

It's Lea...she's dead.

Bubbie:

Toby, I'm Lea!

Toby wipes the tears and sniffles as a hint of breath creeps back into her voice. Suddenly, her smile shines like a Firmadent spotlight.

Toby:

Oh, honey—you look wonderful! I'm so glad you're not dead anymore.

I suppose everyone should be surprised, but this is kind of par for the course for the lot of them. I look at Bubbie, and she's not a bit shaken. It's like she sees past the madness and remembers the way Toby used to be—no matter how much it terrifies her to know how she's really become. Maybe it's those memories that keep them all from losing it. Or maybe it's just nice to be missed.

CHAPTER XX

BLESSINGS

....

The maternité was a memory; the docks a distant dream. Life now was just the moment and the mission to find a rabbi. By now Max was three days old, and in another five he would be ushered into the covenant of the Jewish faith.

Jews weren't easy to find in wartime France. Few ventured far from home, for fear of being seen by strangers or friends. In those days there was no telling which neighbor would sell you down the river for first pick of your dishes and linens.

Trust your own—she had learned that lesson long ago. So, block by block, she searched for those familiar names that had always graced her local storefronts. Long funny names owned by short funny people. Strange, but comforting names, like Greenblat, Lipschitz, Rosenbaum, were all gone—erased from the shopfront glass as if they had been written in beach sand. Her people had vanished; all murdered or hiding like rats in a wall crack.

Europe had changed. The Jewish burgermeisters were gone. The Christian merchants all hid anything worth buying for fear the Reich would seize it. No one went anywhere they didn't have to.

Only the bureaucracy remained steadfast and constant. Upon the close of each month, the *ministre* would summon foreigners to the immigration bureau to have bogus documents stamped by half-blind officials scurrying to clear the country. By strange fortune, it's there that she met a young rabbi who worked as a ship engineer at the docks.

The clergyman-turned-boat-builder was gracious. He welcomed Lea to his home, gave her food and money, and made arrangements for the circumcision of her son. She figured that, even in wartime, tradition should not be forsaken. The rabbi agreed and told her that the Lord would watch over her children, but just for safe measure, he made a blessing over the boy.

He said to gather what he needed and return in five days for the baby's circumcision. Jewish law commanded that ten Jewish men witness the ancient ritual. The rabbi knew four and a trustworthy Catholic.

So, they met with what they had on the baby's eighth day in the dusty basement of the rabbi's house—the rabbi, the mohel,* the handyman, and two soot-covered refugee boys who slept on the coal beside the rabbi's furnace. Shades were drawn. The lights were dimmed. Two candles were lit. A prayer was cried.

Blessed with a few francs from the rabbi, they left to see a woman who the rabbi said would help. She ran a ritual bathhouse called a mikva. The mikva woman knew everything about everyone, and the rabbi was sure she could find someone to take in Lea and the children. The rabbi was right.

As it turns out, the mikva lady had been talking to the matchmaker who knew a fishmonger, who wasn't very matchable—what with him smelling like fish all the time—but this fishmonger lived in a building owned by a retired French actress, and this actress had let a refugee woman stay in the building in exchange for some cleaning and housework.

Well, as luck would have it, the fishmonger took a liking to the refugee woman. Ordinarily, the fish man's courtships ended as soon as he got within smelling distance, but not this time. See, back in Poland, this refugee woman was the widow of the cesspool digger—so to her a man who stank of fish was like a gift from heaven. The couple was married, and to make a short story long, a vacancy had opened in the building.

---

* Man who performs the circumcision. From later investigation we think that this young rabbi who had blessed her son and given them charity was Menachem Schneirson, a man who would one day become the spiritual leader of the black hat orthodox group called the Lubovich—a kind of orthodox Jewish parallel to the pope.

Lea visited the actress—a woman named Claire Dumas. She had retired from show business to devote time to her husband—an important city official who was so important, no one ever actually saw him.

Claire immediately took to Lea and the kids. She sheltered them and gave them an apartment in the building. Actually, it was more like a converted hotel room, but they were comfortable—their hostess worked hard to see that they were. She visited often to see how Lea was recuperating and played with the children. At times she even took the girls outside to the park. The actress loved children and talked constantly about how she wished she could have been blessed with one of her own. She was especially fond of Max. He was a cute baby—pudgy, with puffy cheeks, wide brown eyes, and a fine patch of sandy-blond hair.

The actress held him tightly. She wept as she remembered her own emptiness. "The Lord blesses this poor refugee woman with a child, for what—so the Germans can butcher him?"

FAMILY

As strange as it must seem, my family is really quite close. They've shared a lot of insanity. But, for the moment Grandma Anna and Aunt Pauline aren't speaking to each other again—on account of the Family Feud. Twenty-eight minutes and not a word between them. It's almost as bad as the "Great Price is Right War of '86" when we weathered weeks of their sort of silent treatment.

Anna:
Russel, call your Aunt Pauline for me and tell her to turn on Wheel of Fortune. I ain't speakin' to her no more.

No one is ready for that again. So, Mom has made a peace offering of some bagels and a smidge of whitefish. She knows better than to serve the whole fish. It's common knowledge that, given half a chance, we Jews will devour a whitefish like a school of hungry piranha. But a little snack might get them talking.

In the foyer a commotion is stirring as the stragglers trickle in behind the salty stench of whitefish. At last, there's a chorus for Leon's piano! It rings all the way to the den—obnoxious Russian music echoed by Wink Martindale yapping on the television. It's all just noise to Bubbie. She's had her fill of revolutionary hymns and Mark Goodson-Bill Todman Productions. She's slouched back on our well-worn leather sofa—nibbling and watching, but not listening.

My dog, Rosie, is at her feet. Rosie is short and stout, with a sad, gray face and almond-shaped eyes that speak as clear as any voice. Her blue denim collar is tattered and dons a tag dating back to the Nixon administration. Her once-shiny black coat is patchy and dull.

She has anchored her head on Bubbie's leg. We've told her a thousand times not to beg, but she's too old and too smart to be told what to do. Besides, everyone knows Bubbie's a sucker for an old-timer in need of a handout.

Bubbie:

Oy, vould you look on that face!—So gray, dahling. You're an old lady, like me—eh, Rosie? My old friend. Shhh...here...maybe take just a little nibble vhile no one's looking.

Before you know it, there they are on the couch—two grayheads— sharing whitefish—watching Card Sharks.

Meanwhile, at the breakfast table, Grandma Anna and Aunt Pauline have already forgotten whatever precipitated the whole conflict and are finally speaking again.

Anna:

Oh, Pauline, would ya' look at this! She's got real china all the way from China. Whadda ya' tink she paid for these?

Pauline:

Oh, who gives a shit, Anna?

Yeah, things are back to normal. I guess, no matter how bad it gets, they all still know that family is everything.

CHAPTER XXI
THE PRICE OF FREEDOM

··

It was a dry Tuesday morning, overcast, but otherwise hospitable. Lea remembers it like it was yesterday. You never forget the day someone offers to buy your son. Claire's roses had become overgrown with weeds. So much had been neglected around the building since the fishmonger's wedding. Lea went outside to tend the garden. Claire played with Max. The girls stayed inside to read. You don't ignore your studies just because the whole world is being blown to pieces.

The conversation started casually enough, with the usual pleasantries. You know, "How's your missing husband?"

"Fine. And yours?"

That sort of thing. It was a slow and delicate progression to a bombshell.

"Lea, tell me something. What do you think is going to happen?"

At any other time, that same hazy question could have meant a thousand different things. But not in 1942, not in Marseille. It was understood.

"I'm afraid"—Lea trembled—"Everywhere we run, they follow. I worry that soon there'll be no place left to run."

"Lea, you know what they're doing, the Nazis, don't you? My husband tells me they put the Jews on trains to concentration camps. Auschwitz, Treblinka—no one comes back from these places."

"That's why I run. I stay ahead."

'What happens when one day you're not fast enough?"

"G-d willing, I'll always be fast."

Claire took a deep breath and then let it out. "Lea, I need to ask you something, and I don't want you to be angry with me. Please just listen. I have no children. I've been blessed with so much—I have money, a good career, a powerful husband—but no children. You were blessed with beautiful children, but you are a Jew, which means for as long as you live, the Nazis will hunt you. Lea, you can't run forever. Look around you. They're winning this war. Look at Paris—Hitler marches through the Arc de Triomphe. What will happen to your children when there's no where left to run?" She swallowed another breath and continued unsteadily, "I want you to give Max to me. I'll raise him as my son. No one will ever know he's Jewish. My husband and I will see that he has the best schools, the best clothes—and one day all of this will be his. I'll give you ten thousand francs, enough for you and your daughters to find someone to let you into America. Lea, it's the only way to save them."

What do you say to an offer like that? For a while Lea just stood speechless, thinking. *Could she leave her son to save him—to save all of them? Even if they could run, what kind of life could she give him as a refugee? Would they be out on the street if she refused?*

Lea sobbed and sobbed and then agreed—a quiet nod as she wiped her eyes dry and sniffled. She told Claire she would need a week before she could turn over the baby—for him to adjust. This would buy her time to think.

For days she debated Claire's proposition in her mind. Painful as it was, it made sense. Max would do better with Claire, and the money would get the rest of them out of Europe and away from Hitler.

Lea prayed for guidance. It was a rough and simple prayer. "Lord, please tell me how to help my children." Somehow, even unpolished prayers from the not so pious find their way to G-d's ears, because the next morning Lea knew what to do. They were leaving—all of them—together.

That evening, in the middle of the night, Lea, Max, and the girls set off in search of another home. They were just clearing the gates of the garden when they saw Claire admiring her flowers in the dark. Claire didn't bother asking, and Lea didn't bother explaining.

"In my heart, I wished you could," Claire confessed, "but I knew you wouldn't give him up. You're stubborn that way, Lea—so sure that you can take on the whole world. You have no fear."

Lea quickly corrected the actress. "My fear keeps me running. My fear keeps me alive."

Claire smiled and shook her head. "No, love keeps you running." She reached into her bag and handed Lea some coins. It was just thirty francs, but for desperate people, anything was a blessing. "Here take this and go west to Spain or Portugal. Marseille isn't safe for you anymore."

And with that gift they departed.

CONFOUNDING JEOPARDY

Jeopardy is a game of unrivaled wit—or so say the bluehairs. Like soldiers charging to a trumpeting bugle, they storm the television set and shout desperately for the approval of a hairy Canadian:

Alex Trebek:

Authors for 200. His story of a Cuban fisherman's battle with a giant blue marlin earned him a Pulitzer Prize in 1954.

Anna:

Who is Hemingway?

Pauline:

Don't be stupid, Anna. Hemingway didn't write Moby Dick.

Alex Trebek:

Who is Hemingway?—You are correct!

She smiles glibly.

Pauline:

Oh, go fuck yourself, Anna!

I come from a family of fierce competitors, and the spectators literally drop their business to join the show. Even Leon's piano comes to a grinding halt when that theme song plays. I guess there's just something magnetic about knowing something that the rest of the world doesn't.

But try as they might, this is Grandma Anna's game. It's the one little slice of the day when no one can tell her to shut up. In four years she's never missed a question. Somehow, from exactly

12:30 to 1:00 p.m., a Fulton Street fish peddler with a fifth-grade Brooklyn education has all the answers.

You name it—science, literature, mackerel—she knows all about it. And as I watch the spectacle, I can't help but be awestruck by this pillar of wisdom. And then I remember that this is the woman who told me mushrooms would put hair on my chest and so I scratch my head and wonder how it could be.

Still, we're off to the races, and she's storming out of the gate:

Alex Trebek:

Elements for 200. This element is the primary ingredient in steel.

Anna:

What is iron?

Alex Trebek:

What is Iron?—Correct!

Pauline:

Oh, bite me, Anna.

See what I mean? You just can't shake her.

Alex Trebek:

Famous Families for 300. They were the last imperial family of Russia.

Anna:

Who were the Romanovs?

Alex Trebek:

Who were the Romanovs?—Correct!

Bubbie:

The communists shot that family.

Bubbie knows everyone the communists shot.

Break time. We wait impatiently as Alex concludes his profile of a squatty investment banker from Flatbush. You can see the crowd finally begin to settle, as if they've come to accept that this is Grandma Anna's moment. And then—faster than we can blink—Jeopardy's back.

Alex Trebek:

People in Government for 400. A drink with Richard Nixon in 1966 began the political career of this Reagan cabinet member.

Leon:

Hey, Lea, a Reagan question—you should know this one.

Anna:

Who is Buchanan?

Alex Trebek:

Who is Patrick Buchanan?—Correct!

Leon:

What was Reagan thinking, hiring that fascist? You really ought to talk to him about that, Lea.

Meanwhile, Aunt Pauline still has no answers and is stewing at the thought of being bested by her big sister.

Pauline:

Damn it, Anna! I still think you're wrong about Moby Dick.

Mercifully, at last, they're diverted from their distractions by the start of a new category.

Alex Trebek:

Famous Cities for 200. Napoleon suffered his final defeat in battle at this city.

Anna:

What is Gadolinium?

Gadolinium? We gasp with shock that she—of all people—could miss such a gimme. And as her house of cards tumbles, the next question rolls:

Alex Trebek:

Elements for 1000. This element, represented as "Ga" on the Periodic Table of Elements, is used as a contrasting agent for mechanical resonance imaging scans.

Squaty Banker:

Um...Alex, what is Uranium?

Alex Trebek:

Oh, no. I'm sorry. The answer is Gadolinium. Gadolinium. That'll cost you a thousand.

It's cost Grandma Anna so much more. A gaggle of puzzled Jews stare blankly as the stench of scandal fills the air. Even our host seems to know what's about to happen:

Alex Trebek:

Let's break for these brief words, and we'll be right back for Final Jeopardy.

People want answers. Yet, it's 12:52 and she has none.

A heavy silence hangs as snooty snoops sniff for clues. And there, on the Mexi-Tile bar top, they find what they were looking for. On page 14 of the May 27, 1987, TV Guide, just beside Ed Asner's enlarged head, the ugly truth is pressed in black and white. Jeopardy airs an hour earlier on the Palm Beach station. The reception is hazy but they say if you manipulate things right, it all comes in clear.

Grandma Anna had figured this out years ago and had been stealing away to the study to learn all the answers to life's questions. The yentas* call it sneaky. I say she's smarter than we all thought.

Don't get me wrong. I don't condone what she did. But I learned from Bubbie a long time ago that sometimes you've got to brush aside your conscience and cheat a little to get what you need.

---

* Gossips

CHAPTER XXII
DEPARTURES

······································

Lea did as Claire said and set out toward Perpignan, the last French city before Spain. With the thirty francs from Claire, she had thirty-two francs, not nearly enough for a ticket to anywhere. So by morning, it was time to find help.

Help was Swiss and hid in an abandoned bread bakery fronting memory of a forgotten Jewish neighborhood. They called the place a *consulaire Suisse*—a Swiss consulate. It was windowless, brick, and filled with refugees waiting for money, food, anything the alpine nation could lend. Word was spreading that things would soon get bad. As usual, Claire was right. She always knew when something was going to happen—it was one of the blessings of being married to a big shot.

At exactly 12:45 the relief line stopped at a worn and weary deputy consul scribbling facedown on a clipboard. "Next," he barked in a monotone born only to bureaucrats. "Where are you going?" There was no face—only the crown of a balding head, hanging heavy over the mountain of papers burying a makeshift metal desk.

The young mother stood silent—her eyes fixed on the few surviving strands of hair stretching from east to west across his skull. "Pardon?" she answered, unsure of the truth. "Where are you heading, ma'am?" the scalp said more sternly.

"Spain," she'd decided. Her eyes refused to blink.

The pen stopped swirling, the head lifted slightly, and two marble-brown eyes hoisted high toward heavy eyelids. "Lady, there's no money if you say you're going to Spain, only if you say you're going to Switzerland."

But Lea knew what the line said—the Germans shoot refugees crossing the mountains to Switzerland. And besides, America was the other way. *But if all they want me to do is say I'm going to Switzerland...*

"Okay," Lea answered, "then I *say* I'm going to Switzerland."

The stoic man scowled. A tinge of tone crept into his voice. "It doesn't work like that, honey. We need to know where you're going."

She could see her options had expired. "Look, what do I care where I go," she snapped, "as long as I have money to get my children out of here? These people, they're all going to Switzerland, right? So, I'll follow them."

Again the pen spun and then tumbled to the table. What could he say? It wasn't his money or his neck anyway, so he slid her one hundred francs relief and a small basket of food. It was enough for the fare, so she slipped into the crowd and out the door to the train station. She bought a warm wool blanket and three tickets to Perpignan.

Soon after they left, just as Claire had predicted, the SS stormed Marseille. Roundups surged. One of the people rounded up was Claire. That husband of hers that no one ever saw was finally seen—collaborating with a couple of notorious communists. Rumor has it neither Claire nor her husband survived the war.

BROOKLYN RULES

You wouldn't think it to look at them, but Grandma Anna and Aunt Pauline have been to hell and back. In the days before the fish market, back when Mike the barber gave five-cent flattops, in a place where guys named "Fat Tony" were kings, the Smolensky family faced a brutal decision. Brooklyn was dying. Mighty textile mills crumbled beneath the weight of a Great Depression, and America had barely begun to lick the wounds of a war it never wanted. A proud and powerful nation was out of work.

And there, one icy Tuesday morning, in the bowels of a six-story walk-up in a part of Canarsie you'd never even dream of visiting, Bubbie Smolensky, a stern, teapot-shaped Lithuanian with eyes cold and gray like steel, corralled her four children into her stoveless kitchen to give her solution to the depression that consumed them. Slowly, deliberately, she poured her morning tea—patiently raising and lowering the gray iron kettle, which she heated from the fire of the basement furnace. And then, flatly, but loud above the echo of her pauper's breakfast, she shouted what had to be said. "Children, no crying. You must find work or go. That's all." There was no husband, no money. No other way. The older ones stood frozen with fear—fear of uncertainty, fear of the colossal reality that had been suddenly thrust upon them, fear of the depths of the depression that enveloped them. But in the icy shadow of the young family's silence, Pauline, the tiniest among them, a frail mouse of a child wrapped tightly in a patchy blanket and her sister's shoes too big for her feet, slinked forward and without fear or hesitation squeaked, "I'll go, Mama. For them, I'll go."

For eighteen months she bounced from foster home to foster home, and the family survived. Days and months went by and eventually, she made her way home to better times. But from that first step forward, she was always...different.

Right now she's farting on the couch and shouting at The Price is Right wheel. And though Grandma Anna was the star of the whole Jeopardy debacle, strangely we are all watching Aunt Pauline with bated breath. If ever there was a time for a nasty jab, this was it. After all, she knew it all along. Grandma Anna really was just another fish peddler from Canarsie—just like her. This, my friends, is an "I told you so" forty years in the making.

And so we wait, anxiously studying her as the showcase showdown creeps to a close. But it's our venerable quiz host who asks the question that's on everyone's mind:

Bob Barker:
So, what's it gonna be, Betty? Are you gonna give it another whirl and go for broke or stick with what you've got?

The wheel goes round again, and again we're sure it's coming. After all, this is no ordinary snippet. An opportunity of this magnitude can't be squandered and simply sprinkled recklessly like table salt on yesterday's gefilte fish. It requires concentration. It demands planning. So we all breathe deeply and await the big moment.

Slowly, Aunt Pauline turns a heavy head to her sheepish sister and pensively raises a poorly painted eyebrow. And then, as though the three feet of couch between them were a mighty ocean, she exhales forty years of frustration with a single bellow. "Russel, go get me some ice cubes!"

"Ice cubes?" At least a dozen possibilities swirled through my brain, and all she's got is ice cubes? The scandal she had waited for all her life had just fallen into her surgically lifted lap, and I'm schlepping ice cubes. Mean Aunt Pauline breathed nary a word of it. She just reached for the remote, turned back to the TV, and as she chomped each chunk of ice like a bone-crunching T-Rex, a smoky shout rang out toward the show. Just as the wheel hit *bust, she barked to Bob Barker, "Stupid bitch! See, I knew she shoulda stuck with sixty."*

You know, I had really never liked Aunt Pauline until then. My mother and the others had always adored Aunt Pauline like no one on this earth, and to be honest, I never really got it. To me she was just old and kind of scary. I guess I never understood the razor-fine line between "tough" and "mean." Until then it was hard to believe that this was the person who, without question or hesitation, had come to my parents' rescue with a broom and a checkbook when the beauty shop burned down or gave my Uncle Stanley the money for his first house. She just didn't fit the bill. But I guess in life, people can surprise you—especially if they're lucky enough to really appreciate what they've got.

CHAPTER XXIII
A MOMENT'S PEACE

By midnight Lea had three train tickets to Perpignan—one breath closer to freedom, one step farther from France. Spain sat just across the treacherous peaks of the Pyrenees Mountains—a perilous pass, with soaring cliffs, dense forest, and few trails. She would begin as soon as they had settled and rested.

She set off in search of a rabbi or anyone else who could be trusted to find them a safe place to spend the night, but the children soon complained again of hunger, and again it was time to stop. On a quiet corner in the shadow of the train station, Fanny spotted a small hotel with a pub beside the lobby. Somehow she could always find food if there was food to be found.

They entered quietly in a straight shot to the farthest table. "Stay in back, stay invisible" had long been the way of things since Belgium. They set their satchels beside them and started arranging what they could—papers, clothes, a little milk for the baby. So much to do, it was no wonder that they never noticed the German soldiers at the bar until they were heading toward them.

Lea's heart pounded so loudly she was sure it would give them away. *They know. They know who we are.*

The sweat slowly rolled down the creases of her forehead as the soldiers inched toward their direction. *A calm face—how can I keep a calm face when my heart is beating so loudly?*

"G-d, please don't let them hear it," she whispered to herself, her lips mouthing the words she feared to speak. Her heart pounded. The soldiers continued closer.

The enemy stood above them.

It was as though she had drifted into shark-infested water and hadn't realized it until the hammerheads were swirling the scent of fresh-spilled blood. They were all around, enjoying holiday leave, relishing a moment's peace. They were there—hovering straight above her.

She tried to keep her best game face, sweaty though it may have been. She smiled cordially and then pretended to be busy with her baby. *Shuffle satchels. Fix the milk*, she thought. But three still lingered—staring down. A shiny soldier wrapped in patent leather and polished metal calmly asked in German if he could join them. Lea pretended not to understand. "*Excuséz?*" she queried in her best French. Too much of that Jewish accent would surely give them away. "*Puis je m'asseoir?* May I sit?" the soldier replied in broken but respectable French. She swallowed unsteadily and motioned him to sit. "Oui, Monsieur, allez." Had she refused he'd surely have been suspicious.

The officer was young and nice-looking, tall, maybe twenty, with blond hair and fair skin. His uniform was perfectly pressed and covered with medallions. *Such a young boy to be so decorated*, she thought. She recognized an insignia on his collar—it was SS. She tried to appear unflustered, though in her mind she trembled at the thought of being so near the Gestapo.

"And your husband?" he asked, locked on her shimmering ring. She had forgotten to remove it.

"Waiting for us in Spain." She didn't blink. She started to explain, but he wasn't interested in stories. He was studying faces. He stopped at Max. A smile cracked through stone. "A handsome boy." He laughed as he ran a finely manicured hand over the baby's head. "My daughter in Munich, she's one year like him—a bride for the young groom, perhaps," he joked. "Perhaps," she whispered. "Perhaps," she lied.

But despite the terror, Lea couldn't help but catch a sort of kindness. "You know, they're really very polite people, these Germans, when they're not killing everyone."

The young man reached out his arms, gesturing for Lea to hand over Max. Her stomach spun, but again, she could do nothing to arouse suspicion. She surrendered her baby and watched anxiously. The soldier heaved the boy in the air, *Vrrmm*, like an airplane and then *bzzzzz*, back down again. Up. Down. *Vrrmm. Bzzzzz. Vrrmm. Bzzzzz.* Max smiled and laughed as the young soldier continued to sweep him through the sky. The Nazi and the Jew had fast become friends. Neither had any idea how deeply they feared each other.

The soldier soon tired of games and left as gracefully as he came. "Thank you, ma'am. You have lovely children," he told her with an un-witting smile. Lea knew that minute: time was up.

There was no escaping that they couldn't stay—not another day, not another minute. They had to find somewhere, anywhere, quiet and safe. Discreet wouldn't do. They needed invisible. They needed the farthest corner of the earth.

With eyes scanning all exits, Lea lifted her son and signaled the girls to follow—"slowly, quietly. Not a sound." It was just a few steps away—a light peering through a half-open service door leading to the alley. "Walk, don't run, girls. Head to that door." She'd tread hardly three steps when a hand raked her shoulder. A booming voice bellowed from behind. "Are you being taken care of, madam?" The tone was raspy and female. It was the innkeeper doing her job at the worst of moments. Lea struggled to speak squarely but her concentration fluttered franti-cally between the innkeeper and the battalion at the bar.

The hostess caught on quickly. "Hmmm, I see," the froggy lady mumbled, "Are these your children?"

"Oui, madame."

"And you're alone?"

"Oui, madame. My husband is in Avignon." To anyone in the know that meant the Resistance.

"Come with me, dear, quickly. Back here." She led Lea and the children toward the kitchen where her husband, Claude, a hairy man who stank of grease and wine, was chopping chicken and firing the cook—again.

"Imbecile! Come back tomorrow and see maybe you still have a job—you good-for-nothing!" he shouted toward the clamor in the kitchen. "Such an asshole—this cook! But his brother is a big-shot *milicien Français*, so what can you do? He'll be back tomorrow. They'll all be back tomorrow—German pricks!"

The shaggy man steadied his cleaver and eyed his intruders, *"Que-ce que c'est?* What's this?"

"Claude, *cheri*, these people need help," the matron pleaded.

"Can you cook? Maybe once and for all I can get rid of that piece of shit do-nothing."

"Please, Claude, no jokes. We must do something."

He scratched his stubble and scanned the ceiling. "I have an idea. Come with me."

They followed unsteadily up a service stairway that led to a small caretaker's suite above the kitchen. It was the innkeepers' home.

"This used to be a nice place before Petain gave away the whole country," he grumbled as he lumbered up the narrow steps, "These assholes—they piss on our streets; they take everything and pay for nothing—German swine. And now on the radio this president says, 'Be patient. We must all stay strong and share France's misery.' Such bullshit. They don't know misery. They're all just looking out for their own necks. Keep going...to the back."

A narrow door led to a small supply room in the back of his efficiency. He fumbled for a skeleton key and then creaked it open. "In here. Stay and be quiet. I'll be back soon." Behind them the door slammed shut, the skeleton key tumbled, and in an instant, there was darkness and dead silence.

THE OLDEST TRICK IN THE BOOK

If you'd believe it, I got my literary touch from Grandma Anna. I guess you could say she's always been a master of stories. In her golden years, though, she's been minding my aunt's little bookstore on Forty-First Street. It's the kind of establishment you really don't see anymore—one of those old-fashioned neighborhood shops—dusty, deep and narrow, with used books shelved high all about, though in no particular order. It's a place where an eighty-year-old proprietor sits behind a hundred-year-old cash register greeting patrons by name and telling them what they've got to read. I like to think of it as a snapshot from a forgotten time—an anachronism struggling for survival in a world of fast-food books and multinational megastores. But people still come—straggling souvenir seekers who still long to remember how it used to be in the old days, back when folks had something to say and the joy of the story was sharing it. I guess maybe there's some solace in finding a minute to cherish a lost antiquity. Which brings us back to Grandma Anna and her amazing claim to fame as Miami Beach's most popular book critic.

From Fifth Street up to Surfside, people come seeking her literary wisdom and storybook guidance, which is really kind of funny seeing as she's never actually read a book—not a one. Her eyes are bad, and she has no patience to wade through pages and pages just to get to the twist. So, like with everything else in life, she's figured out a little trick. Early each morning, just before the after-coffee crowd rolls in, my aunt reads her the back cover of every flashy-titled top-twenty she can get her hands on and then the New York Times Book Review about the story. An hour—maybe two—each day they set out to summarize piles of Sidney Sheldons and Danielle Steels strewn about the bookcase shelves and vinyl tile floor. And somehow she remembers it all. Somehow, she always remembers everything.

It's amazing to see. I recall as a kid, some of my fondest child-hood memories were of walking six blocks from school to the bookstore just so I could have my grandma read to me. Looking back, I probably should have thought it strange that with two-dollar paperbacks piled high all around, she never actually had one in hand when she read me a story. She'd say, "Grab a book. Whatcha want me to read ya?"

"This one. This one," I'd squeak.

"What? Cujo?" she'd answer. "Oh, I don't think you're gonna like it, but okay, put it down. Here we go. 'EVERYTHING begins so simply in Stephen King's latest novel, Cujo, perhaps the cruel-est, most disturbing tale of horror he's written yet. One day this 200-pound St. Bernard named Cujo is chasing a rabbit in back of his owner's house, which happens to lie at the end of a dead-end road outside a small town in Maine. . . . When Cujo tries to follow the rabbit into a hole he gets bitten by rabid bats. Pretty soon, Cujo isn't feeling so good. Pretty soon, Cujo is MAD...'"

In an instant, every last customer in the place is mesmerized, breathless, hanging on her every word as they wait in vain for an ending that would never come.

"So, what happened—What happened?" we'd beg. And she'd smile coyly and say, "You'll just have to read the book and find out."

And that, folks, is how she sold 'em.

I never knew. None of us knew. Until I was about twelve, I just figured that every book started with words like "a wickedly funny debut" or "a compelling and suspenseful masterpiece sure to launch him to the top of the charts." I never really saw the reality—or maybe reality was just never that important. What mattered was the stories that sparked the imagination.

Today the story is we have an unsupervised whitefish let loose from the kitchen, and no good could ever come of such reckless-ness. As usual, it's my brother's fault. I guess my brother should be explained—If he could be explained. Actually he's really a hilarious guy. I think being born with the unfortunate name Hymie Wynnowitz Lazega made funny a matter of survival. This time, though, he was careless and left an entire whitefish unguarded on the bar counter.

In no time at all, chaos erupts.

Pauline:
What's that? A whitefish? Pass it down.

The word "please" isn't even an afterthought for Aunt Pauline.

Pauline:
Damn it, Anna! Would ya pass it here, for cryin' out loud.

Anna:
I ain't passin' nothin' to ya', Pauline. Matter of fact, I ain't speakin' to ya' no more.

Auctioneers speak less than these two when they're not speaking.

Pauline:
Good. Then I ain't speaking to you either.

Anna:
Fine, then it's settled.

Pauline:
Fine by me.

Something needs to be done quickly, or we could be here all night waiting for them to stop "not speaking" to each other. Luckily, my brother is fast to the rescue with the age-old art of distraction.

Hymie:

Hey, I think the champ's about to finally lose at Concentration.

Suddenly everything stops as all eyes lock on the television set. After all, everyone in this house knows that a Jewish lawyer couldn't possibly lose to an Irish schoolteacher at this game unless Jamie Farr and the Arabs had the fix in.

Pauline:

Holy shit, Anna! Quick, rub my ass for luck.

We watch astonished as somehow, from zero to sixty, we go from tranquil tension to the unsettling sight of my grandmother polishing my great-aunt's great white posterior like a thrift-store coffee table. And suddenly, like a miracle from heaven, our champion finally sees the light.

Champ:

Alex, I want to solve the puzzle. It's a light bulb.

And with that order is restored. The whitefish slips stealthily back into the kitchen—no one the wiser. Sure, family relations can be thorny. But, sometimes a little diversion is just the trick you need to steer things right.

CHAPTER XXIV

AMELIE-LES-BAINS

A t 4:00 a.m., again the lock tumbled, and the door crept open. It was Claude with a bucket of soap and water wishing they'd wake, wash, and go before the Germans sobered up.

By now, the stupor of schnapps was fading fast, and soldiers were tripping frantically toward empty bedchambers. The strong still standing hovered at the bar, weeping for wives left behind and promising sweet Jesus that they'd never drink again. The shine of metal and leather had tarnished, and all that lingered were boys in wrinkled uniforms, tired and longing for home. For a moment, the great and powerful Nazis seemed…sad.

"Come, now's our chance," Claude warned with a whisper. "We must go quickly." Soldiers were everywhere—staggering the halls, crawling the floors. Those who managed to make it to the comfort of bed left rooms wide open for all to see and be seen.

In their wake, a nervous matron followed swiftly—nudging doors and shuffling stragglers to the pub. "Come, dears," the innkeeper cajoled in her best motherly tone, "let me get you boys a little something for the dizzies. You fellas look like you laid your heads in a pile of shit. Come on, this way. Madame Elyse will fix you up." Slowly, one by one, she eased them to the bar far from sight. "Just sit right here, you poor thing, and I'll brew you my mother's magic hangover miracle."

The matron had a familiar way that made them feel at home. The boys with nickel-plated pistols missed home.

In no time, the path was clear. As quietly as they came, the young family slipped swiftly into the alleyway and headed toward the train station. The rails would only get them to the edge of Amelie-les-Bains. From there no signs would guide them. No road would mark the way. There was only a vast expanse of towering stone blanketed beneath snow-covered pine. To show the route, their host scribbled directions on a napkin, but maps were too confusing so he taught her instead how to follow the stars. He was pretty sure that with a little luck, if they rationed right and rested little, they might not die of cold or hunger before reaching Spain.

CHICKEN SOUP AND OTHER KILLERS

Brunch is finally served. Good old-fashioned burned Jewish home cooking—man, there's nothing like it. The living room reeks of whitefish and blackened cheese blintzes. A fresh pot of matzo-ball soup with chicken chunks and half-sliced carrots boils on Mom's new halogen stove. What was an orderly line to the white-fish platter has broken down and descended into a chaotic free-for-all for the remaining parts.

The bickering sisters go at it again.

Anna:

Why does she gotta put out a fish wit so many bones? She's tryin' ta kill me. Oy, I'll kill myself, Pauline, my own dawta is tryin' to kill me!

Aunt Pauline has another suggestion.

Pauline:

Hey, Anna—

We wait in anticipation, as if maybe she'd say something different—you know, nice.

Pauline:

Go fuck yourself.

Nope.

Anna:

You remembuh Esther Lindbaum?—she should rest in peace. She died like that—I seen it in the paper—choked on a chicken bone.

Pauline:

You ain't seen shit.

Anna:

Jesus, Pauline, why you gotta say such awful tings?

An unusually quiet Bubbie chimes in,

Bubbie:

This vas because she let her son marry a Catholic girl.

We're all waiting for an explanation on this one.

Bubbie:

They don't know from chicken soup, the Catholics. This is vat happens—she should rest in peace—she ate bad soup from a shiksa*. Oy, she was a good woman, Esther. A little stingy, but a good woman. Ach, no, I shouldn't talk about such tings.

Bubbie pulls no punches with the living, but the dead—that's another story.

Anna:

Hey, Pauline, how much ya think my dawta spent on this fish she's tryin' ta kill me with? If I'm gonna go, G-d forbid, it should at least be from a decent piece of fish.

Bubbie's arthritis grows unbearable, and the babble becomes too much. She's been on her feet since six this morning. Brunch wasn't planned until ten thirty, but she was way too anxious to wait that long. So, first thing in the morning, she dashed out to the Jewish bakery to buy a fresh loaf of challah and some black-and-white cookies—soft, saucer-sized cookies glazed with chocolate on one half and vanilla on the other. She wouldn't dream of showing up to my house empty-handed. Bundles in arm, she

---

* Gentile girl

took the number three bus south, then transferred to the number eleven east, and then, finally, caught the K line across the causeway. A microwave she can't figure out, but this she understands.

Right now she's uncomfortable, so she sets out for softer seating. Those metal folding chairs are hell on your back. The pain is strong, and she bites her lip to hide the grimace. It's no use. She needs help to the couch, so I offer my arm. The path there takes us past a room full of gawking geezers with whitefish dropping from their dentures. She hobbles by them in shame, as well-meaning whispers of "Is she okay?" fill the room. She shrugs off my help. "Mine whole life, I do for mineself, and for as long as I'm still here—G-d vilt—I'll do for mineself, for as long as I'm still here."

One creeping step at a time, she inches her way to the sofa... a tiny step..."Oy!"...another tiny step..."Oy!"...a counter to hold...a more ambitious step..."Oy!!!"...the couch at last! She plops to the cushion and throws her arms to the air in a show of victory..."OY, still here!"...a smile.

CHAPTER XXV
THE LONG WALK HOME
··

December 24, 1942. The directions seemed simple enough. They were Jewish directions—follow the constellation that looks like a big soup ladle for about four days across the Pyrenees Mountains until you reach Spain. During the day, Lea just followed the setting sun. There were no maps, no signs, no roads—just an occasional patch of dirt scattered across endless stretches of wilderness and impassable cliffs. They started at daybreak on a rock that seemed to shoot straight upward. A pale December snow glazed the boulder's black shale tip.

In the sliver between stone and shrub lay a broken piece of pine that Lea used as a walking stick and to defend against G-d knows what was lurking in those woods. In her other arm she carried a canvas sack stuffed with trinkets, a half-day's bread, an apple, and a bit of chocolate still left from the relief basket. Dangling from her shoulder was a makeshift water canteen. Like everything else, it was almost gone.

Fanny carried Max. Eva held the end of her mother's dress so they wouldn't get separated. And from sunrise into darkness, they trudged through knee-high snow upward to a peak that never ended. To keep busy, the girls told stories and watched their breath freeze. Lea stayed focused on the position of the sun—and later, the stars.

In daylight it was easy for her to get her bearings—there's only one sun. But, at night the sky was filled with stars—thousands of them— more than she had ever seen in Brussels or Paris. Fanny and Eva were fascinated. They saw roaring tigers—slithering snakes—fire-breathing dragons. "Find me a soup ladle," Lea told them.

There were bears and birds and monkeys, but no spoons. Lea thought, *It all seemed so simple when that mashugina drunk told me to just follow the soup ladle.* But who could find a ladle among so many stars?

So she tried instead to keep the same course they had followed through the day. She studied the tracks behind her, imagining a line extending from their footprints forward to the black horizon. She focused on a bright diamond-shaped constellation at the end of that line, centered it above a distant mountaintop, and with the baby on her belly, forged toward it.

They hiked for hours, stopping occasionally to eat and rest. Lea knew they needed to keep moving, but by early evening their food and water had run out. In the middle of winter on a freezing mountain peak it doesn't take long for three children to get weak and fidgety.

"How much farther, Mama?" Fanny cried.

Eva joined her sister in complaining. "Please, Mama, isn't there anything we can eat?"

Lea looked around at the pinecones and evergreen needles—surely something here must be edible? There was nothing. Maybe a drink would settle them. She told them to take a handful of snow for their thirst. They all knew they shouldn't eat snow, but they did it anyway. It was all there was.

The wind nipped, and the frost bit, and by early evening there was no going farther. By now the girls' shoes had great round holes, and Lea's stomach had swollen like a balloon from the weight of her load.

So, they settled alongside a large boulder, with the rock faced into the wind to help shield them from the sting of the cold winter breeze. No hut, no tent, no cover except the rock and a large blanket that the four of them snuggled under. Lea wanted so badly to make a fire—anything for warmth. Her father had told her how the Indians in America used to make fire by rubbing sticks. She wouldn't dare try. The light and smoke would surely give them away to the patrols below. So they snuggled beneath the blanket—waiting, listening, shivering.

It's an unbelievable quiet, the Pyrenees at night. You'll swear you can hear moonlight. A dead silence, cracked only by the occasional cry of a wolf or squawk of a bird foolish enough to brave the bitter mountain winter. It's a vast wilderness swallowed by the blackness of a cold mountain sky.

Beneath a whispering moon, they huddled in the darkness, lulled by the listless crackle of a cold December wind. A calm had finally started to settle when a snap in the brush shattered their stillness. Someone was coming. "Shhh. Don't make a sound," she warned the girls as she covered Max's mouth. Even the baby knew by now that there are times to be quiet. Their hearts raced as the fluttering in the brush drew closer. Lea craned her neck from beside the rock. She could make out a light in the distance—it was a man. They waited, paralyzed, listening to the sounds of their heartbeats and the snapping tree limbs growing louder. Then their silence was broken. Max began to cry. At first it was a few peeps—"Ack–em. Ack–em." Lea pressed him harder to her chest, hoping to muffle his cries. It was no use. The baby began to wail.

A raspy voice cried out in French, "Don't worry, I won't hurt you." Maybe it was his tone—maybe it was because he was French, maybe it was because they just couldn't run anymore—but for some reason, Lea believed him. She slowly crept out from behind the rock, baby in arm, trembling before the man who found her. She could finally see him in the dim light of his squeaky oil lantern. He was a tall, burly man with the start of an impressive beard. A large canvas sack that he hauled with no effort was perched atop his shoulder. Gently, he set the bag on the frozen ground, and removed half of a baguette, a stick of salami and a fresh bottle of wine. "*Mangez, mangez*. Eat, eat," he said as he broke a large piece of bread for Lea, who divvied it into smaller pieces, which she passed around with the wine bottle. Even Max had a bit to drink—to settle the nerves.

The stranger invited everyone to keep eating, while he bundled sticks for a fire. "No, no fire!" Lea cried. Her voice trembled as she struggled to soften her scream. "We're refugees. The soldiers will see."

The man was steady. "I know your story. Trust me, we'll be okay. It's Christmas Eve, the Germans will all be in church or drunk." Again, for some reason there was something so familiar and settling about him, so she agreed to the fire. Besides, if they didn't warm up soon, frostbite would set in, and they'd be dead in the snow anyway.

The warmth and light of the fire were heaven, though the wine may have helped, too. The girls shared scary stories about horrible man-eating creatures, some of which were probably prowling the woods around them. Lea and the stranger talked of more sober matters—directions and unguarded pathways. He said he was a salt smuggler and that he knew the safest routes across the mountains. He had been slinking back and forth between Spain and France, sneaking salt into Perpignan. It was dangerous work, but someone had to do it—now more than ever at eight francs a pound.

"Come, we must go now," was all he said. Embers flickered in a circle of shale, but just like that they were hiking again toward Spain. Lea hoped to rest for the night but there was no time to sleep. Patrols were never far, and they'd need to reach the summit by daybreak. The stranger just felt it. He pointed to a light miles off in the distance. It was a church at the tip of the mountain. Up there they could rest.

For a while he followed, balancing little Max on one shoulder and his satchel of salt on the other. Then he handed the boy to Fanny. Moments later he was gone without a word or a trace. He just vanished when they came within sight of the church. The girls wondered how he could just disappear without the slightest sign. As far as Lea was concerned, there could only be one explanation—the angel she carried on her shoulder had come down for a while to return the favor.

They knocked on the rickety church door, just like the salt-smuggling angel had told them to do. A young nun, amazed at the sight of the rag-covered refugees, opened the door and quickly escorted them inside. Midnight mass was nearly ending, but the family's unexpected arrival cut the service to a sudden end. The priest rushed from his pulpit to tend to the shivering young mother and children as black-gowned nuns crossed themselves and whispered of miracles. This time of year, the Catholics were particularly sensitive to mysterious infants appearing from nowhere on the doorstep. "It's the miracle of Jesus," they cried. Lea thought, *You want to know from miracles, I should tell you my whole story.*

The priest asked how she found their little church. She explained that she met a salt smuggler who had fixed a fire and showed them the way through the mountains. The priest knew nothing of this smuggler. Again, the nuns crossed themselves. The priest explained, "Many, many refugees have been captured or killed trying to cross these mountains. It's truly a miracle of Jesus that brought you to us safely." Their miracle, her angel's miracle—at least somebody was looking out for them.

The nuns pitter-pattered closer and draped the children in blankets. They laid the baby on a rickety church bench, changed his rags, and guided the group to a dark cellar with a small fireplace kindled in the corner. It was home for the night.

Sleep fell heavy until daybreak, when the sisters woke them to get moving. Word would soon get out about the refugee family hiding in the church.

They led Lea to the door and pointed her down a path toward a little house about two days' walk from the Spanish border. It was the last house on the French side of the mountains—no more than a day from the little church.

Lea and the children left quickly. They needed to seize as much daylight as possible. By nightfall the bristly path would be slow traveling.

They set out walking deep into the night—groping their way across mossy rocks and dense underbrush. Eyes down—always. One wrong step on a narrow ledge would send you tumbling down a mountain.

To keep busy, the girls finished their stories—Hansel and Gretel this time. They pretended the pebbles reflecting in the moonlight marked a path home—left by a cute little blond-haired Dutch boy who would save them from witches and buy them chocolates. But a rock is a rock—no matter what your imagination and a bit of hilltop moonlight might tell you.

Fanny and Eva wanted desperately to follow their shiny trail. They begged and cried, but Mama had her own course—one that took them through snow so thick you couldn't see any glittery rocks. They tried to explain about Hansel and Gretel and the pebbles and the witch, but Mama was too busy looking for stars to worry about witches and rocks.

Soon the stones were gone, and there was nothing but snow. The girls scoured the ground desperately, searching for any hint of the trail that their little blondie had left them. A faint reflection cracked through the ice. "Such a strange rock?" Fanny wondered. She brushed the snow from the stone and began to shriek.

Lea squeezed her mouth to quiet her.

"Mama! Mama!" Fanny tried to scream, her cries muffled by her mother's icy hand. She pointed with her eyes, struggling to explain what was at her feet—a human skull, a nameless casualty of a bloody Spanish civil war not quite over, lay unburied on the frozen ground.

Lea followed her daughter's eyes to the ground and then calmly started the girls walking again—this time more briskly than before. "It's only a rock, girls. It's only a rock," she assured them. They all knew better but had to believe it to keep going.

Hearts racing, they pushed on until nearly midnight, when they finally reached the little cottage—a rickety shingle cabin with a sharp-pitched roof and a smoky chimney. They approached cautiously, tiptoeing up the creaky pine porch steps. A rotted handrail broke loose in Lea's hand. She glanced for witnesses and, as soon as she was sure the coast was clear, tossed the banister beneath the stairs. For a moment she stood motionless, drawing slow, strained breaths as she waited to find her composure. Then, finally, she summoned the strength to knock.

The girls trembled as their mother gently tapped the door. Horrible images of goblins and monsters raced through their minds as they recalled their stories from the night before. "Mama, this looks like a witch's house," Fanny cried. Lea told her to be good. A crooked old woman with a long, hooked nose opened the door. Her head was draped in a red babushka. Her shriveled face was dotted with horrible shadows cast by her flickering oil lantern.

The girls' eyes bulged. "Mama, she's a witch!" Fanny whispered in a panic.

What with that house and that nose—even Lea had to wonder.

But the crooked woman greeted them warmly and led them inside past a small group of refugee boys—teenagers—asleep in the corner on the living room floor. They dreamed quietly around a large stone fireplace where an oversized kettle boiled a red Spanish soup. As they passed the fireplace, the girls nervously studied the cauldron, wondering which of them might be first to cook in it.

Quietly, they tiptoed across squeaky planks to the old woman's bedroom. "You shouldn't have to stay out here with these boys," the old woman creaked. A shaky hand pushed open a narrow door and guided Lea inside. "You and the children can share my bed."

She was an odd little woman with an odd little house. Everything there was a twist of proportion. The cabin was small; the woman, downright tiny and the furniture enormous. The dressers, the bed—everything looked like it was made for a giant. A family of six could have squeezed into that bed, but luckily they were only four and a witch, so everyone slept comfortably that night.

Morning came with a sharp rapping of a cane against the bedpost. It was four o'clock, and the boys were already gone. "You need to go quickly," the old woman warned. "It will be light soon, and the soldiers will be out."

Refugees don't tempt fate by lingering. They grabbed what they could and hurried out the door. Every minute mattered.

For two more days, they trudged through slush and mud down the slippery mountainside—actually they slid and fell down the steep cliffside a lot more than they walked. It was a long and tiring downhill trip. Their sore legs trembled with every uneasy step down the icy rock face. But by December 28, they had nearly reached the bottom. Spain was in sight.

STRENGTH

Bubbie hasn't been feeling well these days. Her right arm hangs heavy from last June's stroke, and the doctors say her cholesterol level is off the chart. But still, she manages to make her way.

Bubbie:
Look on this—I can barely move now—me! I used
to climb mountains, and now I'm like a cripple. I
haven't got the strength anymore. No, no more—
I'm not the same Bubbie.

I never know what to say when she gets like this. I try to sell her a bit of two-cent advice just to have some sort of reply.

Me:
Maybe you should see a doctor?

She gives me a look that makes me feel like I was born yesterday. At seventy-seven years old, she sees more doctors than a Jewish widow on the hunt for a husband.

Bubbie:
They don't know nothing, these doctors!

A shout of comisery rings out from the den.

Anna:
You're tellin' me! My docta charges me a hundred
and fifty bucks just to tell me nothin's wrong.
Would you believe the nerve?

Pauline:
For a hundred and fifty dollars, you'd think
that prick could at least say you got cancer or
something.

158

Bubbie just tunes it all out. Her thoughts are buried in that last bit of grainy decaf swirling at the bottom of her Dunkin' Donuts mug.

Bubbie:

No. No more doctors. Those phony baloney HMO bullshit artists. They gived me pills—Oy, so many pills! Red pills, blue pills, yellow pills—who knows from all these pills? I vas so sick from all this medications. I throwed the whole ting out and now—now I feel a little better. See, your Bubbie knows better than all these shysters.

I hopelessly try to interject,

Me:

But Bubbie, you really should—

Bubbie:

You remember they send me last month to the hospital to make again the operation for the heart. Ach, they put me in a room mit a voman, she must be like a hunderd three years old. I never seen nothing like this. All night this roommate screams—"Let me die! Let me die!" She keeped screaming and screaming. And they don't do nothing, these doctors. The machines go Bip. Bip. Bip. And nobody comes! Finally, the middle the night, she shuts up, and the machines stop bipping, and a schwartze nurse who takes care on her runs in mit the doctor to vake her up. Every time she's finally quiet, the nurse schleps the doctor to vake her up. I don't know vhy she can't just leave this voman to die in peace. I tink she must really need that job, this schwartze nurse, that she should keep this voman alive like that. Ach, not me. If, G-d

159

*forbid, I should be like that voman, the only doctor
I vant you should call is Doctor Kavorsky.*

Me:

You mean Kavorkian?

Bubbie:

Ya, that's the one!

Swish. Swish. She wipes her hands clean of it.

Bubbie:

That's it—finished. Goodbye, Bubbie!

I almost think she finds a certain strength in lamenting her
weathered condition. There's a lot of things I think but don't have
a clue about. Still, she seems so alive as she's talking now. I see
that fiery spark she once had. 'Once had,' 'Used to'—G-d, we say
that a lot about her these days. So much feels like it's slipping
away. What gives her the strength? Christ, what gives us the
strength?

Bubbie's quiet again—sipping stale coffee, noshing on strudel,
and watching some sort of quiz show that she can't figure out how
to change with the VCR remote. My sister-in-law has followed to
the couch to rock her newborn child to sleep. He has my father's
round face, and Bubbie shines when she sees him. She reaches
to hold my brother's pink-faced boy for the first time. Her arms
are weak, but her smile is strong and wide. "All right, so let it be.
Vat can ve do? Listen, I'm not so young anymore. At least I live
to see blessings like this." Her arms wobble as she strains to take
the infant from his nervous mother. Suddenly, she's strong again
as she plants a kiss on his wrinkled forehead. "Oy, such miracles
that I live to see! These beautiful children. My great-grandson!
Okay. Vat can ve do? Look, I'm still here. I'll manage."

She always manages. Same old Bubbie.

CHAPTER XXVI

SPAIN

·················

Spain: beautiful, filthy, sweet, pungent, magnificent, foul Spain. You could smell the blood of the revolution that had ripped through the quiet kingdom, scattering trails of beggars and stains of misery all along the quaint countryside. But right now, there was no place on earth more beautiful.

Descending that mountain, Lea felt like Moses on Sinai—a half-rotted sliver of pine for a walking stick; a frostbitten face aged thirty years by four days of winter; and the beckon of a war-torn promised land at her trembling feet—feet that finally surrendered their long battle with the ground beneath them. Hardly a hundred meters from the dirt road into town, she collapsed. The clothes, the trinkets—all that they carried, save the immigration papers and baby—scattered along the Spanish mountainside. Luckily, Fanny still held Maxie, so Lea could schlep the bundles. She kept him wrapped tightly in a blanket, which she tucked snugly inside a laundry sack turned baby sling. Only a tiny nose, bright red from the cold, peered through the spindle of well-wound wool and canvas.

On the dusty ground, a battered mother with swollen legs cried for relief, but there was none. Even war-worn children are ill suited for such situations. Eva wept. Maxie chewed his fist.

Fanny studied the landscape. *Somebody? Anybody?* she thought as she made a mental note not to cry. *Don't let the children see fear.* Without blinking, she shushed her sister and raised her to her feet. "Eva, stay here with Maxie," the near-teen ordered with almost-grown-up confidence. "I'll go get help." The fatigue of climbing made it hard to walk and left her hobbling like a polio child. But still, she pressed on.

She scrambled through strange streets in a frantic search for help, as her mother lay half-conscious at the foot of a conquered rock. She begged and pleaded, tripping awkwardly toward town, but no one would listen. After all, for the moment she was just one more panhandler—French, no less—with a story no more pitiful than their own.

Behind the church, beside a rustic bar, a beat cop chased local drunks from the alleyway, swatting garbage cans with his nightstick. "Come on, let's go! You can't hide from your wives forever," the lawman grumbled.

Fanny saw salvation. *"Au secours! Au secours!* Help! Help!" she cried quite Frenchly in desperation. But the policeman stared blankly—unmoved and unsure. "Go on. Move along!" he barked. "Find someplace else to beg." This one had seen groveling children a thousand times before. "I said move it"—he prodded again—"there's nothing for you here." Fanny reached and clawed for the words, but soon saw that she didn't need them. A frantic scream from Eva in the distance shattered the language barrier. The cop soon hurried to the spot where their mother lay facedown on the ground—her cracked lips glittered with dust and bits of gravel—the tips of her mouth dotted with the blood she'd begun to cough.

In broken French, the policeman promised that he'd take them safely to a hospital. But Lea knew that hospitals mean paperwork—paperwork means bureaucrats—and bureaucrats mean deportation and a ticket straight to Auschwitz. "Jail," she cried. "Please, take me to jail."

It was the safest place she could think of with food and showers.

The officer was puzzled. "But, señora, you haven't done anything."

She repeated again, strongly and surely, "Take me to prison. Take me to prison. You can find a reason later."

So, with the girls and an infant in tow, Lea was arrested and brought in for disturbing the peace and illegal entry upon Spanish soil. She would celebrate her son's first birthday in jail.

The policeman took them to Comisaria San Pau, a hospitable jail by wartime standards—a dryout for local drunks mostly. The jailhouse was gray and stank of urine. The guards marched mother and children to processing past prisoners who rattled their cages and cried foul.

"You got the wrong guy," a perpetual prisoner pleaded. "Man, it's a bad case of mistaken identity."

The guard rattled back with his nightstick. "Yeah, Nacho, we mistook you for some other drunk we found passed out on the street."

Processing was cold and swift. A woman with a face dark like an eggplant with bloodred lips took their information. "*Nombre?* Name?" she asked as she clicked away at her typing machine. She kept on typing, though all Lea had told her was her name. "And the children? The little one, too." Again, a lot of typing for such short names. Clickedy, clickedy, click, RING. Clickedy, clickedy, click, RING. Done. "Go with the guard." They had been processed.

Next stop was the fingerprinting and photo room. One at a time, the guard lined each of them up against a measuring wall. "Hold this number under your chin," the cop ordered as he escorted Lea to the X chalk marked on the floor. Click. Click. Flash. "Okay, next." One by one, their pictures were shot against the numbered backdrop. Even Max was measured and photographed. The guards stood him against the wall and held the prison number below his chin—Click. Click. Flash!—Inmate number 472 was a menacing seventy-eight centimeters tall.

Fingerprinting followed the photos and was spun from the same circus. The guards somehow had the not-so-bright idea that they should record everyone's prints—including baby Max's. They inked his right hand and tried to coax him to make a print on the intake card. Well, needless to say, they got the prints they wanted—on the desk, on the wall, on their clothes—everywhere. By the time they managed to stop his clapping and print the other hand, the guard, the desk, the baby, and the paperwork were all a mess of streaks and smudges.

The painted guard returned the spotted baby to his tired mother and motioned them to follow to the cells, where sorting was to start. Max was still nursing, so he stayed with Lea. The girls were sent with the nuns to an orphanage.

Lea tried to reassure herself. "The sisters will take good care of them for a while." It was little solace. Despite being busy with Max, her thoughts always strayed to the two who couldn't be with her.

But the guards were kind, which helped. They brought bread and cold tomato soup and asked Lea what she wanted for the baby's birthday present. She could think of only one thing—a bath. The policemen obliged and hauled in a large bucket of water and a bar of soap from the washroom. A full-blown circus large as life wouldn't have impressed that child as much as that dented tin bucket and soap. He splashed the soap bar into the water, laughing as he soaked his mother. His chubby face and wavy hair were covered in soapy suds. Even the drunks in the tank were amused by his antics—other than an occasional fight, nothing exciting ever happened there. They watched as the usually quiet child blurted his first word, *"Agua!"* Over and over he echoed the crowd as he continued to splash. "Agua! Agua! Water! Water!" Clearly, he was impressed with his gift.

Lea couldn't help but think. Ten years ago she had given her daughter a doll for her first birthday. It was beautiful—French porcelain with dark curly hair and a dress she had made herself from a patch of real silk. This year, it was a miracle she could give her son a bath. Funny thing is, Max would have taken that clanky bucket over a new toy any day of the week and twice on Sunday. Somehow, children, in their ignorance, understand and appreciate miracles a lot more than the rest of us.

The euphoria of the birthday festivities quickly wore off, and reality soon set in. The prisoners resumed their clanking, while the guards chattered about what was to become of the young mother and her children. "They'll probably ship 'em back to France," seemed to be the general consensus. But they had come too far, and suffered too much, to be sent back now.

Lea scavenged for a way out of the jail she had worked so hard to get in to. "A priest!" she cried. "Please—quick—call a priest! I think I'm dying!" Being good Catholics, none of the guards wanted her eternal damnation on their hands so they raced to the nearest church. Lea knew that a man of G-d would be more sympathetic than a bureaucrat or cop.

In a miraculous moment, emergency salvation was quick to the doorstep. She explained to the young father that they were Jews and that they would be sent to the camps if they were deported. At that point she wasn't exactly certain what the camps were except that no one—not Mama, not Papa, not Claire's friends, no one—ever seemed to return from them. She begged him to contact the American consulate and the HIAS. The priest made the sign of the cross repeatedly and chanted in Latin as he discreetly listened to her plea. In between "omnibus" and "pluribus," while the guards weren't looking, he whispered that he would do as she asked.

Two days later, representatives from the church, the HIAS. and the American consulate were at the jailhouse. With that kind of support, the guards had no choice but to let her go—what between a priest, a rabbi, and a bureaucrat, they'd have been damned to two hells and an eternity of paperwork if they didn't. Within an hour of the rescue party's arrival, Lea was released and returned to her children—no more legal a resident than she was the day before, but she was free and reunited with her family. And sometimes, when you've lost so much, that can be all you need.

BURYING ABRAHAM

My uncle Abraham died a couple of years ago. People came from all over to pay their last respects to my bubbie's brother. I don't know that he was a particularly popular guy, Uncle Abe. He was bald, kind of gruff, and had this peculiar accent that made him sound like a James Bond villain. But sometimes, it's just time to close old wounds and lay bitterness beneath the earth. And this must have been one of those times.

Don't get me wrong, he wasn't an unpleasant man, Uncle Abe. He was just a bit odd. He'd make air-conditioning by strapping ice cubes to a desk fan, and he covered a vintage motorcycle with wallpaper to ward off rust. On a sunny Sunday afternoon you'd see him on it—a crusty old man roaring southbound down Collins Avenue on a "harvest wheat" BMW.

And then, of course, he had this irrational distaste for Syrians. Not all Arabs, just Syrians. I'm not sure that he ever actually met a Syrian, or why the line stopped at Damascus, but that's how he felt. He'd rant, "Ach, this Syrians—you can't trust them for nah-ting. They tale you someting on Tuesday, and it's no good on Wednesday." And whenever he'd say that I'd wonder whether at that very moment some old coot on the back stoop of some alley in Abu Kamal wasn't venting that what the Jews had "taled" him on Wednesday was no good on Thursday. But, I suppose, for better or worse, that's who my uncle was.

He was Bubbie's big brother, and really, in many ways he was better to her than we ever could be. I try to visit from time to time on my way to the mall. My father fixes the cable now and again. But, Uncle Abe—every Sunday, like clockwork he'd start his weekly spin with breakfast at Bubbie's. In a tiny yellow kitchen, atop a rusty gas stove, she'd fix him watery tea and burned omelets.

And he'd smile half-toothless with his mouth full of crunchy eggs and say, "Nobody cooks like you, Lea." For years this is what he did—Uncle Abe never missed a visit with Bubbie.

So I suppose that's why it pained Bubbie that her brother's children had become so distant. I'd hear her moan, "Oy, that Leon's got such a big mouth! Ach, and his sister—vhat a cheap-skate! I never seen somebody so stingy! Mit all her millions—so much money that husband left her—and she still schleps across town to shop in thrift stores—mit coupons! And never once in all these years does she invite me up to that fancy-schmantzy apartment of hers."

There's the real source of her bitterness.

"Not once does she say to me, 'Tanta* Lea, come to my house and share some tea. Tanta Lea, come visit my home. I'll make you a nice plate of soup.'"

It's a simple matter, really, but in a Jewish family these are the things feuds are made of.

So, for ages we'd rack our brains to figure out what it would take to finally bury the hatchet. But nothing ever seemed to make it right.

And then a funny thing happened at my uncle's funeral. My cousin slunk across a room full of well-wishing mourners, threw her arms around my grandmother, and invited her to sit shiva** in her home. There, thirty-five sobbing Jews devoured whitefish as they thumbed through black-and-white memories of the man and his wallpapered motorcycle. And with that, all was forgotten.

In the Bible they say that when the Great Patriarch Abraham died, it was the first time in decades that his children—two distant brothers—were finally united. In the far-off fields of Machpela,

---

* Aunt

** Jewish mourning ritual. For seven days, friends and family come to the home of the bereaved and sit with them for support.

beneath the dusty stones of a desolate desert cave, Isaac, the father of the Jewish people and Ishmael, the father of the Muslim people, embraced and buried their common past.

I guess Uncle Abe was kind of like that—laid to rest with a hatchet in the coffin.

CHAPTER XXVII
VIVA LA REVOLUCIÓN

H ome for now was the police captain's car—a rickety but otherwise accommodating '37 Peugeot—white-walled and black with wood-paneled doors and a pine crucifix standing sentinel above the dashboard. For tonight it was somewhere to sleep—a place to rest until things got better.

By now, waves of refugees had begun slithering through Sau Pau along the same broken path as Lea. They had started at Perpignan, made their way across the mountains to Sant Llorenc de la Muga, from there transferred to Figueres only to wind up at the jailhouse in Sau Pau—stuck between countries—trapped between lives.

One behind another—twenty to a cell—they packed the prison and slept on stacks of hay while slow-moving Spaniards stood waiting for orders from distant commanders too busy surviving a revolution to tend to petty administrative matters. "Leave it for Fulanito," they'd say—which everyone knew meant "let it languish."

So the word was just to wait. But waiting always seemed dangerous. This war had a way of dropping bombs on the grounded. Still, the sanctuary of a warm sedan and the blessing of a day's cold soup seemed a better plan than most. So they laid their heads on the wagon's broad benches and slept a sweet sleep they'd forgotten since Albi. Tonight, at least, jail was safe and sound.

—w—

Morning broke with the ruckus of the roll call. Squawking guards and squabbling prisoners crowded the commissary as the smell of sweet tomato toast crept its way to the one-car motor pool. At the front of what was fast becoming a chow line, a boorish jailer barked for order.

"Gomez, Pablo! Gomez, Pablo! Step forward."

"It's 'Your Majesty King Pablo the Fifth' to you, Sergeant," the prisoner quipped as he shuffled his feet slowly toward the chow trays.

"Ah, shut up and move it, Gomez. The priest is here for confession, and I'm sure you two got a lot to talk about. Go on, get going—back there. You can eat when the Good Lord's gotten his due."

At the rear of the commissary, a familiar clergyman pushed and squeezed his lanky frame through the cattle call toward a makeshift confessional. His long bony body waved a holy bible high above the crowd like an episcopal signpost. His slender shape slithered through the unruly mob, skirting contact and ducking confrontation.

"Hey, Sarge, you better watch out for that priest," Gomez was quick to quip. "On Sunday he wants your money, and Monday he's asking for your soul. Ain't that right there, Padre Pine Tree?"

The priest was green enough to be shaken and wise enough to stay quiet.

"Come on, Gomez, quit razzing the padre," the cop cracked as he pointed a billy club past the gazpacho. "It's not like you've gotta be afraid of him, anyhow. Long as I can remember you ain't had a nickel to steal or a soul to save. So I guess it's not gonna cost you much, eh? All right now, move it. You can get your food after you tell your story to the priest."

"Hey, lady," the prisoner shouted from across the commissary to the young mother and infant, "you see what they do here? They control you. First they take your mind, then they come for your soul. You tell everyone what's happening if you get out of here. You hear me? You tell them."

The sound of a nightstick clamoring against a steel prep station shortened the show. "All right, knock it off! Get moving, Pablo—excuse me, King Pablo. This nice lady don't want to listen to your foolishness. Why don't you go on and give the church a challenge and see if they can find a soul in you to save." The cop drew in his belly and softly waved a hand toward the breakfast line. "Si vous plait, Madame...this way."

Lea started toward the soup and then suddenly stopped. She turned to the cardboard confessional and whispered to her translator.

"Sergeant, one minute, please," the interpreter interrupted. "The woman wants to speak with the priest."

"The priest? Well, there's a few here who need him more than you, lady, but be my guest. Father Antonio, over here!"

The priest was tall, dark, and skinny and looked like he jumped straight from the seventh grade to the seminary.

"Yes, my child. I see you're feeling a little better today?" he asked in broken but passable French. "What can I do for you?"

"Do you know what's going to happen to us?" she asked flatly. It was a practiced question. It was the only question.

"I don't know, my child. I don't think they know. Last night another fifty arrived from Figueres, and every day it's more. No one has answers. We're Catalans. I think everyone just figures we'll just build a bigger roof to put over you."

"Father, can you help us get out of here?"

"It's hard to say. Things are complicated here right now. Besides, where will you go?"

"That way," she pointed through the iron-barred window away from the rising sun, "I'll go to my sister in America. We'll keep moving west until we get to my sister in America."

"Go with G-d, my child. Believe me, He doesn't stay much around this place."

—⁂—

What lingered in the comisaria was chaos. But Spain was a place that understood chaos. Last year these people were Catalans. The year before they were loyal subjects of a deposed king. This year Madrid said they were fascist revolutionaries at war with the king, the Catalans, and anyone else the great general ordered them to hate.

But still, strangely, it felt like home—at least it would need to be home until they could start out west again. For now, just a thin paper wall held the Germans east of Andorra. But it was only a matter of time before Hitler would trample another nonaggression pact; merely a question of when the sound of stomping boots would ring through the quiet streets of Spain. Moving—running—was the only choice. But Madrid didn't say to run; they didn't say you're free to go; they didn't say anything. The capital was silent.

"Father," Lea asked the priest quite impenitently, "we are all stuck here in jail, but where is the sin? Why can't we go?" But I guess the question was never why—it was where. Where do we put hundreds of hungry people when we can't even feed our own? After all, by now Spain already had its fill of limbless veterans looking for a roof and a cane. Caravans of needy Jews could only mean more misery. But still they came, and still Spain waited. Every day welcomed more desperate wanderers with their lives in satchels and bony children clasped to their thighs.

All that was left were the people in the salvation business—the church and the HIAS—and their troughs were dry. What Franco hadn't commandeered for the cause, the desperate stole for survival. "Go south," they said. "All of you, go to Barcelona if you want to eat. Go to Barcelona if you ever want to leave this place."

CHAPTER XXVIII
LOVING BARCELONA
IN THE RAIN

....

Spaniards live for two things—to dance and to fight—on some days at the same time. It was a ravaged and bitterly poor country but also a land of unprompted passion that tenderly tapped the unending extremes of the emotional reservoir. It's a place she'd have never left were her whole world not a gunship-guarded ocean away.

She had settled on the seedier fringes of Barcelona, in the heart of Catalonia, along the Caldes de Malavella, in a borough called Banys Nous. You could see it from the surrounding mountain range—a wondrous place that looked like Christmas—a fairy-tale town of mushroom-shaped buildings with snow-painted rooftops—evenly spaced and cut round at the corners. Broad boulevards dotted with mosaic houses shot like spokes in all directions from the town center. Rainbow-colored lizards of concrete and glass spit water into great stone fountains. Random hedges pruned like fantastic animals crept up from caged courtyards. Barcelona was a postcard—yet strangely, backward: sidewalks sliced through the center of the roadway; the funeral home was pink; the church seemed an unimaginable black with lance-like spires that pierced a smoky sky waiting to gush rain. The family had at last found heaven—a gingerbread paradise tucked quietly at the foot of a majestic mountain.

Like everything in those days, the first move was to sort out friend and foe. "Start with your own," they'd say. And if you can't find your own, find a church. The church wasn't hard to find. Her great, gray cross towered tall above the gothic quarter as a seven-hundred-year reminder that, in these parts, faith was still the center of everything. Faith, that day, marked refuge from the approaching squall.

It was an unseasonable rain in an unseasonable time. Mostly it poured from above the mountain peak and gushed down the old Roman roads that snaked down from the summit of Montjuïc washing through the granite alleys of the ancient gothic town. From the shore a mist slowly rolled ahead of a thunderous rain. Storms were converging from all sides.

At the steps of the ancient church, a legless woman with a leathery face too old for her years sat weeping on a mat of straw. Her brittle hand shook a cigar box of coins and reached for pity. *"Algo de comer?*—something to eat," she groveled, *"Cinco hijos—cinc fils*—five baby." In this place they could beg in so many languages. Back in Belgium, on the right day, if the kids weren't fussing, and the mood was right, Lea might have stopped. But now there was nothing. "I'm sorry, but I'm no better off than you," Lea answered as she brushed the raindrops from her children's hair and huddled for shelter beneath the beggar's tent. But the withered woman scowled and snapped, "Look! Look at this!" she said as she hiked her dress to her shriveled breasts. The stubs that remained of her legs were raw and badly stitched. *"Joder!* You have more than me," the old woman barked, "Give! Give!" A family's last three francs tumbled to the ground.

By now the rain was settling, and Lea could at last see light. Pigeons pacing the courtyard scattered swiftly to the rooftops as lines of workmen scurried single-file through the chapel, lugging lumber and satchels of fill to an unfinished annex in back of the church.

The church, like the Catalans, was a work in perpetual progress—under constant construction—with building scaffolds towering high above the belfries, and sandbags scattered all about the sanctuary. They said they'd never stop building her—their great gothic beast—a testament to the unbreakable patience of her conscientious craftsmen.

When they're not fighting and dancing, the Catalans live to work. They're industrious and gritty—a people in motion. Nothing was ever finished and a new project always waited on the horizon. "It gives you something to do tomorrow," they'd say. But this day was Wednesday. And with work to do and not a saint to celebrate, the church was miraculously quiet.

The aisles seemed dim and devoid of a soul who could help. There was just an old woman, alone, kneeling and weeping in a church pew. The weeper was gray and frail and looked as though food had forgotten her. Lea approached gingerly, "Madame, are you okay?" she instinctively asked in French. The old woman thought to smile and then thought better. She seemed to defend her misery as though it were the last thing she had left in this world. "...*en el nombre del padre, el hijo, y el espiritu santo, amen*," she said to the cross and then slowly turned to Lea. A watery eye lifted and looked. "You're French, no?" the old woman creaked. The light of relief softly peeked through her tears—like being from somewhere else—anywhere else—had to be better. Lea replied unsteadily, "Belgian, but we were living in France." She dared not give the whole story. Even here, with all their problems, people could surely still find room in their hearts to hate Jews.

But the old woman was gracious, in a "G-d save the Queen" sort of way. She crossed herself to say goodbye to Jesus and then said her name, "I am Mrs. Castillo." She gave no first name, and from her ancient form it seemed as though she never had one. Slowly, she rose from her sorrow. "My husband, Christ rest his soul, was French—from Perpignan. Do you know Perpignan?"

"Oui, Madame, I've been."

"And these are your children?"

"Oui, Madame. I am Lea," she whispered as she hoisted the baby from the puddles they'd steadily dripped to the ground. "This little mouse is Max. And these are my girls. Go on, girls, introduce yourselves." But the girls just stared straight upward, hypnotized by the lofted ceiling that pointed straight toward the heavens and the brilliant organ pipes that reached like long brass fingers balancing the roof. All around, caged cloisters draped in dancing candlelight seemed to stare back from all sides—the peering eyes of priceless treasures—gilded angels blowing trumpets of war, silken cherubs locked in bloody battle, portraits of heaven itself ripping apart. Mystical had its own meaning here.

"Well, go on girls," Lea nudged with a bit of a blush. "Stop gawking and say hello to Mrs. Castillo." But the magic of this church was overpowering. Fanny slid back to the moment and curtsied. *"Je m'appelle Fanny*—I'm Fanny." Eva just stood fixed on the images above her and muttered her name, *"Eva. Enchanté,"* she mumbled, never looking past the wonders around her. Lea was quick to correct. "Eva, up straight and proper! Mrs. Castillo is speaking to you." Eva straightened herself, got out *"bonjour"* and a halfhearted curtsy and then turned back to the soaring stained glass and the gray stone, walls that seemed to melt into random shapes and spit concrete people from all directions. This place was no world she'd ever known.

Without words there is no work. So, Lea reached for help. "Mrs. Castillo, can you teach me to speak Spanish," she pleaded. The old woman looked her up and down and answered frankly, "My dear, before you can speak like one of us, you need to look and sound like one of us." Lea stood confused—not knowing where to start. "How do you mean?"

"That coat, child, it looks like…well, you look like the mortician's widow. We've got to find you something with a splash of color—maybe a Gitana scarf with a dash of red. And shoes…Oh, dear, yes, shoes. And we'll have to do something about your name."

"My name?' she answered.

"Well, of course, darling. It makes no sense at all here—sounds too Russian. I think…Yes, I think we'll call you Lila. Okay, Lila, what do you want to learn?"

"I need a job, so teach me what I need to work."

And so the old widow started by teaching her to say, *"Yo trabajo. I work,"* and the Catalans understood that.

CROSSWORDS

I love my town! Miami is a colorful place where everyone is from somewhere else, and no one speaks the same language.

Anna:

Hey, what's a eight-letta word for perplexed...starts with "C"?

Leon:

смущенный.

Pauline:

What'd he call me?

Leon:

It's Russian—It means confused.

Anna:

I ain't confused. I'm just tryin' to figure this ting out.

Pauline:

Why don't you just make a list of words until you find the one that fits?

Bubbie:

No lists!

Bubbie's got this thing with lists...they kind of freak her out. I remember a couple weeks ago she came with me to pick up my mom's car at the repair shop. It was no big deal—a little stick in the gears that just needed checking—but she went along for the ride.

It's a nice dealership, and we made ourselves comfortable in one of those fancy customer lounges where they serve gourmet coffee from plastic push-button machines. I sipped watery vanilla hazelnut decaf. Bubbie entertained herself reading wall signs. She's got this habit of reading things out loud as she sees them. "Disney World—96 miles"; "Billie's Alligator Heaven—Oka...lu... skee exit. Oka...Vhat...ski? Oy, vhat kind of name is that? That guy don't look Polish to me."

Truth is, it used to drive me crazy, the reading. But then I stopped and thought about the wonder of it all. How on earth did she figure out how to read this stuff? She has barely a fourth-grade Polish education. English isn't her language (or even her alphabet) but there she goes..."Schedule A service $199.99—Ach, so much money?"

"Credit cards...this line only"

"Volvo five star service..."

She shakes as she reads the "Volvo" sign and then turns to me quickly.

Bubbie:

Volvo? That's German, no?

Me:

No, Bubbie. Volvo's Swedish.

Bubbie:

The Germans don't make this cars?

Me:

No, Bubbie, it's a Swedish car. The Swedes are okay. Their only crime against humanity was Abba.

Bubbie:

You're sure this isn't German?

Me:

Positive, Bubbie, please...

Bubbie:

*No. No. I tink I remember I seen on the television
that Hitler made this company.*

Me:

*That's Volkswagen, Bubbie—not Volvo. There's no
problem here with the Jews.*

We're fast interrupted by our service adviser—a heavyset Cuban
guy with a thick accent who calls himself "Poopie." Poopie greets
us warmly.

Poopie:

*Welcome to Mi-jami Volvo. I jam Poopie. Please put for
me jew nem on de list, and I come right back for jew.*

Oh, no. Bubbie turns pale as I reach for the clipboard.

Bubbie:

Don't give them your name. They're Germans!

She hardly notices that Poopie the transmission tech is far from
a field marshal.

Me:

*Bubbie, technically, they're Swedes. Now can I have
a pen, please?*

Anxiously, she scans the exits and then questions once more the
big "Volvo" sign above the service counter.

Bubbie:

*Are you sure this company aren't Germans? I tink
I read somevhere that there's a case mit them and
the Jews.*

Me:

*Bubbie, there's nothing going on here with the
Jews.*

Poopie's back with some disturbing news.

Poopie:

Listen, I need for jew maybe three days. Jew got a problem with jew axhol.

Okay, now he's over the line.

Bubbie:

Listen, Mr. Poopie. This is America, and I don't have to be afraid from nobody anymore. G-d blessed me that I live here now—in America, the greatest country in the world, the home from the free.

Poopie:

Jew right. I lov America.

Bubbie:

G-d bless America!

Poopie:

Si, G-d bless the Jew-Ass-A!

And with that came peace and mutual misunderstanding. I guess somewhere along the way our crossed words take form, and somehow, in spite of ourselves, we manage the miracle of communication. I never really had that struggle, so I suppose for me it's a little hard to grasp—this idea of reaching across the table to someone from another world and making them understand you. But Bubbie has lived that battle her whole life—Poland, Belgium, France, Spain—the Jew-Ass-A. Through her travels she's managed to pick up five languages ("English from vhich she speaks de best"). And while we sometimes feel there's no getting through to her, I think in the end, she always manages to find the words she needs.

CHAPTER XXIX
HOME SWEET HOMELESS

The bitter winter months brought a need for coats in the North and the hands to stitch them in the East—where working hands were plentiful and cheap. But these were different days, when times were tough, and everyone just understood that good jobs go to good Spaniards. But in war everything changes.

Allegiances were few, and friends were fickle. Spain had been severed from her neighbors by nonaggression pacts and ripped from Europe by her own revolution. After four years of bloody civil war, General Franco had nothing left to offer his neighbors but his neutrality. And while neutrality made no enemies, it also made no friends. So Spain was now a forgotten peninsula left to limp and lumber alone.

Maybe it was better—to be forgotten. German memories were long and unforgiving. And what they didn't remember they wrote on lists. So, for now, it was best to stay out of the way—to be "just a tree in the forest" as Mrs. Castillo would say. Besides, folks on the Iberian side didn't care who you were if you were quiet and didn't ask for help.

Help in Barcelona was the HIAS, and the HIAS was tired. All they could scavenge was tales of salvation and crowded quarters on the fringe of Girona, an old border town with a storied history of harboring wayward Jews. But far from town meant far from freedom—two trains from any consul and three buses from city hall. Though, I guess, for now, it was as good a place as any. And so, for now, I guess they'd stay.

Money came from the Jewish Joint Distribution Committee. Who they were and what they distributed was anybody's guess. They were

Jewish and willing to lend a hand. That was enough. And really the JDC was quite good. They opened soup kitchens twice a week and offered provisional housing at a shuttered hotel downtown.

By now, refugees had started lining up one and two families to a room. A caravan of calamity had settled on the south side. But Lea knew that too many Jews in one place could never be good if anyone ever decided to point a finger. So they settled instead on a small boarding house on the outskirts of town.

The boarding house was dark and damp with a long dim hallway lit by the faint glow of cigarettes. Dirty men with crutches and canes lined a narrow corridor, blowing smoke and waiting for nothing.

"Lady. Lady. A few pesetas for a wounded soldier, please?"

"Help a poor cripple, would ya', miss?"

Cries for charity echoed through the crumbling corridors. Pleas for pity groaned from every curtain-covered doorway. Deep in the distance, you could hear flannel-draped matrons clanking copper pots and shouting something about getting a job.

"Psst." A sound swished from a dim-lit doorway. A shadow flickered. A cigarette simmered and belched smoke into the hallway.

"Hey, sweetie," a voice hacked through the smoke in broken French toward Fanny, "what's your name, pretty girl?"

"Fanny," the girl answered, more from reflex than mere fear.

"Fanny. That's nice. I like you, Fanny. Why don't you come let me show you something upstairs."

The child gasped, motionless, locked on the stranger's pointy moustache that seemed to reach upward on one side whenever he'd finish a sentence. "I don't think so. My mom's waiting for me at the check-in. I'm sure she's looking for me."

"Come on. Just for a minute. I've got a kitty cat. He's upstairs. You want to see him?"

"No. No. I really..." she stammered as she searched for an exit. Everything at that moment seemed wrong. His soot-stained brow dripped sweat to the floor. His tongue cleared the edge of his shrubby moustache like a cat cleans its paws. In a flash Fanny's feet started swiftly toward the door. The rest of her quickly followed.

"Mama! Mama! Let's go. We can't stay here. Come on, we need to leave," she gasped nervously as she tried to tug her mother toward the exit.

"What is it, Mamala? What happened?"

The young girl leaned and whispered to her mother's ear and then pointed a finger toward the figure peering through the smoke at the end of the hallway. It started as a walk toward the shadowy form, and then a gallop, and then a stampede. Three swipes of her canvas satchel across his forehead was all it took. "Stay away from her! Stay away from her! Stay away from her, you animal!" The commotion called a crowd and an angry wife. Her language was incomprehensible, her fury with her mate—crystal clear.

"He won't bother you again. Now get your things, girls. Come, our room is this way."

—⁂—

It took just three days for the baby to feel sick. At first, it was almost unnoticeable, a slight cough—Ack! Ack!—quiet, like a faint whisper or humble protest. But each day it grew louder and longer—stronger than the baby that nursed it. The sickness found strength in a place where the idea of medicine meant call a priest because a doctor was slower and charged twice as much.

Of course, priests are never hard to find in a place that's starving for salvation. And this priest had answers, "I'm sure of it. I know what this is. I've seen it before—*la pulmonía*, we call it—'the pneumonia.' Oh yes, the boy definitely needs a transfusion. We can fix this. It's all in the blood."

"Blood? Whose blood?" Lea jolted from reflex.

"Not to worry, my child. There are donors. The doctor will explain."

"Explain what? My baby isn't getting any transformer."

"It's a transfusion, my dear, and he might die without it."

"Well, if he's getting blood, it's not going to be anyone's but mine."

So it was settled. A needle was drawn from cot to cot—arm to arm. Mother and son were joined by blood. And that would fix everything.

Soon, the baby started to settle. The fever slowly broke. The congestion gradually cleared. His cantaloupe-shaped face at last worked a smile.

A PICTURE IS WORTH
A THOUSAND MEMORIES

Bubbie has what you might call a sort of obsession with smiling pictures. Her pink floral-papered apartment is completely covered with them. The canary-colored kitchen that doubles as her entrance foyer has a whole bunch neatly framed in old plastic-wood discount pharmacy frames and dozens more scotched-taped up and down the vintage avocado fridge. They're happy moments—scattered Polaroids and family flashbacks of special times...weddings, birthdays, bar-mitzvahs...a place where the whole crazy clan is suited and dolled up in their finest. It's a place she always likes to remember.

Scamper three steps to the living room and there's more...lots more. Montages of memories are nailed to every wall. Pressboard collages, with photos slapped one on top of the other, are tacked to every sheet of wallboard in the house. Cousins, children, grandchildren, great-grandchildren all beam back from high above the shag rug forest as if to say we're here with you.

"Sit. Be comfortable." Have a seat on the plastic covered sofa and you'll see even more of them. Piles of lavender, peach, and pink photo books cover the imitation antique French coffee table like a pharmacy-photo bridge that spans the decades. It's a tableau of sloppily pasted pictures stuck half-sideways into faded, spiral-bound picture books. Their striped, plastic pages tell the checkered story of a long and mostly-joyous life.

But in the bedroom is where you'll find her most prized trea-sures. Really it's a bit stark and kind of somber—A simple box-spring bed, a beige easy chair set to the side and a white vanity mirror perched on a chipped brown dresser. The mirror's border is a scotch-taped frame of snapshots and stills—Kodak memories of people loved and long gone—her parents, her brother and sis-ter, a daughter taken way too soon.

This retro-chic place is a collage of her life—a time capsule of the continents and decades she's walked—her story in black and white and faded color.

It's funny. This thing with pictures must have caught on be-cause my aunt's also crazy about them. She loves them so much she even went on to start a successful art and framing gallery. I remember her being so proud when the business first took off that she rushed over to Bubbie's place with a magnificent piece hand-signed by a terribly famous painter. Picasso, as a matter of fact, I think it was. An entire entourage came by to help hang it where the whole world could see the signs of her success.

Gently, my uncle moved a pressboard photo gallery to the closet, measured the wall and displayed this new masterpiece square and dead-center above the sofa. Bubbie, politely kissed her daughter, said "Tank you, Dahling. It's lovely" and the fol-lowing week when I came to teach her how to use the answering machine, Picasso was in the closet and my bar-mitzvah pictures were back up above the sofa.

"The painting vas nice," she said almost humbly, "but I missed mine family. Listen, a blue ox mit two heads? That's this guy's *story. Not mine." Seconds later she found her smile and a perky pitch as she nailed another cardboard photo album to the wall, "This!" she cried as she blew a kiss to her photo-graffiti wall, "This is mine story!"*

"You know it's such a pity," she said to me as she rested her hammer on the end table and returned to the moment, "I got a neighbor Doris on the fourth floor—you remember her, the nice lady mit the crazy clown hair. Anyvay, vould you believe that this poor voman don't got any pictures in her home. Nahting... such a poor, poor lady. So, I take pity on her 'cause she must be so lonely not to have any photographs to keep her company. I bring her food. I come play cards mit her. Me, I'm never lonely. I've got all this beautiful pictures." A heartfelt kiss again blows toward the west wall of Three Seasons Condominium, Tower 3, Unit 503.

They say, "a picture is worth a thousand words." Maybe when you've lived such a horrific and wonderful life it's worth a lot more—like the marvel of knowing that one glimpse can make you cry when you need to remember or make you smile when you need forget.

CHAPTER XXX
A TIME TO LAUGH

··

"Smile, Eva. The man wants to take your picture." It was like a dream, only mostly in Spanish. There they were on the stage of the converted theater. A drum-beating band blared in the background. The boys stood tall and proud in their finest church suits. The girls twirled like spin tops draped in ribbons and ruffles, with lips painted far brighter than they ought to be. Somehow, the world seemed at peace in the tumult of a rumba.

Three weeks and two food riots had ticked by since they'd holed up in that horrid hotel. But finally Eva had wheedled her mother enough to believe that three hard-begged pesetas would be better spent on fiesta night at the Catalonia Club than food. But the truth is they needed to live like the locals; they needed a normal kind of crazy; they needed to dance.

A flash bulb flickered before the tiny dancer could even clear a quarter turn. "Perfecto! That's perfect!" An accented photographer queried from behind a boxy Kodak camera, "May I take another with you and your lovely mother?" But the girls quickly smiled, giggled, and then ran to chase boys. "Come on, Eva. Let's go"—Fanny jostled her sister—"That one back there is cute, and he's got a brother that's perfect for you." Eva just winced. "Fanny, you're so boy crazy! Well, I guess we need someone to dance with."

Meanwhile, the stranger stayed and snapped another shot of Lea. "Absolutely lovely!" he cheered as the flashbulb flickered. "Come see me after the show."

She stared with a look somewhere between confusion and concern.

"The picture. Come see me at the end of the show for your photo," he said with a coy smirk. "Don't worry...this one's on the house. No one's really buying tonight anyway."

The stranger seemed polite enough—sophisticated and troubled—like an important man who had tumbled from high atop a perch of money. He also sounded rather...foreign. Like them; but not like them.

The bearded paparazzo abruptly broke unbreakable ice. "So, where are you from?" It was a horrifically innocuous question, and one they couldn't answer.

"We're staying here in Barcelona," she cautiously responded. "And you? Where are you from?" She knew that accent sounded familiar... troubling.

"Originally, Vienna." Her heart stopped beating as she instinctively scanned for a pistol. "But now, I'm here. Just me and my camera. We're simple now...hawking pictures to people with no money and selling memories to those who just want to forget. You know, I used to have a nice business back home...Even with the Nazis...Especially with the Nazis. They wanted pictures of everything. But you know how these things go. You have...And then some pig with a day-old government badge wants to take. So now, here I am—not smart enough to make a deal, I suppose. Oh well, I never much cared for the whole '*Deutschland über ales*—Germany above all, Heil Hitler' thing anyway. Hate is like fashion to these people—like bowler hats—one day everyone loves them—the next day they hate them. And then eventually they throw it all in the trash and move on to loving and hating something new. We Austrians were always the bastard stepchildren of the German people anyways. So it was just a matter of time before they started loving and hating us. I knew that one day soon I'd be next, and it was time to go."

The man paused and looked quietly to the commotion on the dance floor. "So, do you know how?" he asked somewhat smugly. The young mother stared blankly, unsure if she understood the question. "What do you mean?"

"The rumba. Do you know to dance a rumba?"

Again, she stared blankly.

"Well, then I have something else to offer you…some lessons," the accented stranger said as he hoisted her up to the dance floor.

—ഝ—

The next morning came the mail run again. It was always the same. Pass the abandoned storefronts. Pass the beggars at the veteran's center. Pass Pepito's newsstand. All that seemed to linger from this revolution was the hope for news of better days to come.

"Hola, Señora Lila." a small sound squeaked from behind a tall stack of newspapers, "How's your Spanish coming along?"

"Hola, Pepito," she answered in her best-practiced Castellano. "Where in the hell are you?" Pepito was tiny and tough to find.

"I'm back here loading up the rest of this bullshit propaganda that just came in. Can you believe that these Fascist assholes expect me to sell this crap? Our glorious government took everything that anyone would want to buy and sent me this—Franco's fat face on everything. Look, they've got posters: 'One Spain—The Great General will unite us!' There's postcards, 'The revolution is forever!' and now they're even making Franco comics for kids. Thank the Blessed Virgin for my stash of French pinup girl pictures, or I swear to you, I'd starve. I tell you, Lila, it can't go on like this. We Catalans are being raped by this revolution—if they don't kill us—they take everything for 'the cause' and leave us cold and hungry. I hear there's still a few Basques kicking the Great General's ass up in the mountains. I think I'm ready to grab a gun and join them."

"Maybe soon, Pepito. Maybe soon," she answered, her eyes drifting to scan the few Spanish words she could make out from the day's headlines. As usual it was more of the same—"Franco this" and "football that"—rigged politics and staged sports. But like most days lately, her mind traveled far from the battlefield that Pepito longed to charge. Four months of hoping and praying hadn't managed to bring her an inch closer to America. Maybe today things would change. Maybe today good news would come. And then, right there, in the faded caption of the Sunday *Sentinel*, between a Saturday soccer score and a weekly arrest report, she spotted what looked like the words "refugee" and "children" and swiftly ran for a two-centimo coin.

"Mrs. Castillo! Mrs. Castillo! Please come read this! Come read it!"

"Lila, Lila. Calm down. Let me see."

"I need to know what it says," she asked again, unable to steady her breath as she fumbled for her change.

"All right. All right. Let's have a look, child," the widow answered as she reached for her spectacles, "Goodness, you're so impatient, girl. Well, come on, let me get a look at that..."

Then the old woman lowered her eyes, held her breath, and smiled.

CHAPTER XXXI
A RESCUE FROM ROOSEVELT

· ·

"**E**leanor Roosevelt is coming for the children!" the sound rang like a symphony. The words floated like a dream—like Humpty Dumpty or Alice in Wonderland or one of those other fairy tales you're taught to believe when you're too young to know better. It was all so unexpected and fantastic it couldn't possibly be true. But the newspaper said it—and the newspaper only lies in Moscow.

It was really there, plain as day, in the subtle shadow of the day's big soccer story: Madrid 3, Barcelona 1.

AMERICAN FIRST LADY TO RESCUE REFUGEE CHILDREN

America's First Lady, Mrs. Eleanor Roosevelt, is expected to arrive in Lisbon this April with an unexpected surprise—safe passage to the United States and immigration visas for 50 European refugee children. The children will be selected through an application process with the U.S. Department of State and must have relatives or foster families in the United States to receive them...

It was a kernel of hope for the hopeless, but it was all they could ever dream. And just like that, she was off to Lisbon racing to lead the list. Day after day she'd pace the ministry's mahogany-walled vestibule to the point the consul couldn't stand it anymore. "Señora, please go home. Nothing has changed since this morning," he'd demand with the unbreakable smile of a varnished diplomat. "If I hear news of a ship

192

coming to take people from here, I promise you on the grave of my sainted mother, you'll be the first I call."

Back in Barcelona it was no better. "I don't know anything about any list, but not to worry, señora, as soon as I do, I promise, your family's name will be on it. Now go home and wait. We'll contact you if we hear anything."

After two and a half months, the word finally came. Her children were heading to America. The visas were only for children. So Max, Eva, and Fanny would have to go alone with the nuns. At fourteen months old, Max was the youngest passenger. It would be Fanny's job to care for him now until they reached their aunt in New Jersey. Lea still couldn't get immigration approval from the United States. But at least the kids were safely on their way to America. For now, Lea could only wait.

COMISERY LOVES COMPANY

Bubbie:

*Did I ever tell you the story from how I got papers
to come here to this country?*

I'd heard a zillion stories, but strangely, never that one. So, I lowered my bagel, set the lox on the coffee table, and listened with earnest interest.

Me:

No, Bubbie, I never heard that story.

Bubbie:

*I had an uncle Opper, a tailor, who came here from
Lodz before the war. He vas a nice uncle, but a
little strange. Vell, one day a crazy friend of his,
a Russian, vas teaching him this ting that they
jump from airplanes. How do you call it?—sky
jumping? Oy, only Russians vould tink of such a
tings. Anyvay, he gets so excited from this sky
jumping, my uncle, that he starts putting together
these parachutes. He'd go around like a beggar to
all the other tailors looking for extra silk to make
these shmatas.* He had boxes and boxes of them
and kept them in back of his shop. Everybody
says he's crazy—"Vhat you gonna do mit all this
parachutes?" But he kept making more and more.
And then the war started, and everybody vants
parachutes. They're calling him from all over for
these tings. Ach, he made such a fortune selling
these shmatas, and so he gave a little money to
somebody to help me get the visa.*

---

* Rags

Me:

I guess you were pretty lucky, huh Bubbie?

Bubbie:

Ya, lucky. But it vas different back then—ve all helped each other. Today—everyting is "Me. Me. Me." In my time it vasn't like that. This uncle didn't know me, but I needed help, so he wrote letters, gave money. So many people—even strangers— opened their homes for us, brought us food vhen ve vere hungry. Today you don't open your door for nobody—they kill you. I don't know. Maybe— ve needed each other more back then. Ya, it vas different then.

If I didn't know better, I'd say she's nostalgic for the bad old days— like she longs for a simpler time when everybody knew exactly why they were all killing each other. Or maybe, it's just as plain as the notion that shared struggle is still something shared.

CHAPTER XXXII
THE FORTUNATE FIFTY

···

"Come, come, children. Come aboard," the Sisters of St. Francis chimed in a sing-song that rang music to the ears. "Just let us know if you're hungry." Somehow, three years of hungry leaves you unsure where to start on a statement like that.

They'd launched from an old boatyard in Lisbon—a half-abandoned port lined with rows of stranded cargo ships—merchant vessels frozen by the finances of war. But the SS *Serpa Pinto* was different—alive, moving, and cleared for passage. Fifty liberated children were free and heading west.

Though they'd seen boats, none had ever seen anything like this. Hordes of tiny refugees scampered with amazement while overwhelmed and outnumbered grown-ups rallied for order. Girls giggled. Boys bounced. Unshackled childhood joy shrieked through the corridors.

"Let's go children. Boys to this side. Girls to that side. The baby can come with us. Come, come, children. Let's go. We need to get you cleaned up for supper."

The nuns were compelled by clean. They offered fresh clothes, scented soap, and a hearty delousing, and then scurried the youngsters off to their cabins to await the dinner bell.

Freedom was a phenomenal commotion. Sorrow washed to smiles. Children reclaimed a youth stolen and innocence lost—racing up and down the narrow corridors and laughing to their hearts' content. Eva bounced and danced on her bed until her head spun. Fanny dreamed of boys who looked like Andy Hardy. They had nearly lost what it was to laugh, almost forgotten that the world was coming to an end.

In the hazy shadow of a dim-lit hallway, a boy, lean and hairy and almost big enough to ride a motorcycle, put a sudden stop to the celebration. He peeked a pointy nose inside the cabin and then at their luggage. "Let me see what you've got in there," he ordered, trying to figure what to take. The girls stared blankly, unsure whether to fight.

"What are you deaf or stupid?" the bully badgered once more—his point blunt and unbending. "I said hand it over."

Outmatched and outsized, the girls lowered their heads and reached to their satchels. There was nothing left to take anyway.

But then, in a flash, a squeaky voice echoed from the hallway. "Hey, leave them alone, meathead. Why don't you go back to Siberia, or wherever you're from?" It was a hero to their rescue. He was older—maybe even fourteen—and dashing, with slicked-back sandy hair and a sharp tie. A smaller boy stood at his heels like a faithful cocker spaniel.

"I said leave them alone, moron," the brave boy ordered. But the badger wasn't budging.

"Why don't ya come over here and do somethin' 'bout it, twerp, and see if I don't sock ya one," the bully barked without blinking. This wasn't his first confrontation. It wouldn't be his last.

But their defender stayed steady. "Take a look, meathead. There's two of us. And then these two. And one of you."

The math was indisputable. The battle over before it had begun.

"I'm Herschel," their hero turned and said with a smile, "and this is my friend Solomon. I think we're going to a place called Pittsburg—to stay with Soli's cousin. Where are you heading?"

Fanny blushed and gazed doe-eyed, "Um...We...We're—" Eva quickly leaped forward with a fearlessness that only fades when boys start to matter. "We're gonna stay with our aunt in New Jersey—my sister, Fanny, and me."

Fanny was fast to chime in. "I think New Jersey is near Pittsburg."

The boy chuckled and winked. "Fanny, eh? I guess we'll see you at dinner, Fanny."

Fanny smiled and managed to squeak "okay" as he strutted toward the dimly lit stairwell.

"Oh, Eva, do you think he's handsome?" she sighed as she watched him trot down the corridor.

Eva grimaced and dropped her jaw. "Uck! He's a boy—with dirty fingers."

"Eva, come on. Help me do something about this dress. I can't have Herschel seeing me like this tonight. See if you can find me some scissors and thread. I'll make a minidress just like Lili Damita or Betty Davis. It'll be positively sophisticated." It was positively...lopsided.

—w—

At six o'clock the call to dinner came. The place was filled with magnificent meals. Long-forgotten delicacies like oranges and lamb—and some dishes they couldn't even pronounce—were spread all about the linen-covered table and set on crystal and silver.

At the head of it all was Dr. Sequera—a tall Portuguese pediatrician who had friends with friends with a hand on the government stamp. He had cashed in his favors and then borrowed a few more, to manage a miracle for fifty children he didn't even know. It was the most magnificent kind of medicine.

—w—

Fourteen days at sea. Turbulent seas that spit straight in the eye of a gusty march wind. By the third dizzying day they had reached the great green isle of Madera off the coast of Portugal. Madera was a magnificent, mountainous place where towering terraces of rock hovered high above a crashing coastline and forests of laurel filled the cavernous valley below. Beyond the emerald grass a great baroque church leered over the vaulted cliff-side and down to the vineyards that the nuns had carefully tended for centuries. This was a happy place, naturally...one bottle for the winery. One for the sisters. One for the winery. One for the sisters. Until the sun set over that glorious green mountainside.

YESTERDAY'S PAST

"Exquisite! A stunning example of post-modern sculpture with a hint of Greek and Phoenician influence." Uncle Erwin has finally arrived! We're halfway through brunch, but he'll scramble to bless what he can and still somehow find time to critique the latest artwork.

He's smart, Uncle Erwin, cultured and learned in the old ways. He knows all about stuff like art and history and Phoenicians. Dad says he's from the old school—steeped in philosophy, tradition, and a dozen other things that have fallen by the wayside in my CliffsNotes culture.

He's a slight man, really, my uncle, excruciatingly Hungarian, dressed to the nines, but otherwise quite charming in a Count Dracula sort of way. It's funny—you can hear him whenever he rolls in. He's got one of those grumbly Eastern-bloc accents that just rings through a room:

Erwin:
Grrrrreetings, distinguished counselor.

The Rs rrrroll from his tongue. Firmly, he takes my shoulder and guides me to a lonely bronze sculpture perched atop a marble pedestal in the foyer.

Erwin:
Tell me, dear nephew, what do you think of this piece?

Uncle Erwin always asks you the question before he gives you the answer.

Together, in a rhythmic swoop, we scratch our chins and circle like buzzards scouring for a weakness. "Truly magnificent!"

he cheers as he kisses his fingers. "I found it for your mother in Thailand. It's by a Croatian artist. The poor man's a lunatic, really—terrible tragedy—he wanders the streets naked to get his vision, but his work is brilliant."

Again, I circle and try to study it as he does but just don't see it. To me it's a vulgar statue—a screaming, naked, bronze woman dangling from a crescent moon. But to Uncle Erwin, she's fascinating. He understands that the artist's message isn't nearly as important as his pain in expressing it.

"Notice the lines—the agony on her face. Magnificent!" he cries as he runs his fingers along her bronze bust, clueless that he is molesting our furniture. To the "world's largest dealer of bronze and rare sculpture," she's just raw materials fused and pounded into an expressive contortion. To me that expression looks like something from the late-night shows I used to watch through a scrambled cable reception. But Uncle Erwin sees right past her to something more, and his enthusiasm draws a crowd.

Suddenly, he's joined in his rotation by an unlikely trio: Bubbie, Uncle Stanley's gay cousin Stanley from New York, and his English boyfriend. Each feels obliged to pitch his two bits.

The Englishman puffs, "I see a Greek influence."

Cousin Stanley sees it, too. "Yeah, definitely Greek."

Talk of ancient peoples intrigues Bubbie, and she cries, "They used to feed people to the lions—these Greeks."

So there it is—Art History 101 brought to you by the bubbie, the count, the queen of England, and the queen of Queens and I rush to scuttle this discussion before someone puts two and two together and comes up with a number I'm not prepared to deal with.

"That's the Romans, Bubbie. I don't think the Greeks fed their enemies to anybody."

A shout rrrings from behind the bronze: "They threw them from cliffs as sacrifices to Poseidon," explains Uncle Erwin. And after careful deliberation the scholars unanimously concur that this is what happened.

"You know, in France they used to kill people mit a guillotine," Bubbie adds. "Whoosh, off mit the head! But I guess vhen I vas there during the var that vas too much vork so they just shot everybody or gave them to the Germans to shoot. The Russians shot everybody, too, but they vere better than the Germans. Oy, such a terrible ting—you can't imagine."

Then, it suddenly hits me—this is the world she left behind—a place where killing was an art, and people prayed to be rescued by Bolsheviks. But though she recalls those days with sadness, strangely there's really not a hint of bitterness. It's more like a glowing sense of accomplishment—like deep down she's quelled by the knowledge that survival is sweet satisfaction.

I don't know. Maybe I should be confused or shocked by it all but, to tell the truth, I just feel a little disconnected. I haven't lived enough to see much history. When I was a kid, Bubbie would teach me the French stories she learned in Belgium—about how they pissed in the fountains and chopped off the queen's head so they could eat cake. But I've never really understood the past. My world of cornfield caucuses and "drugs for arms" scandals is just so different, and when she says things like "you can't imagine"—I suppose I can't.

CHAPTER XXXIII
WAIT FOR WORD

··

B arcelona, Spain. Nearly every day for fourteen months brought the same routine. Bright and early stroll past the beggars and then on down to the consulate for the latest wave of paperwork. Say hello to Mrs. Castillo, who's out on the church steps complaining about how bad things are since Franco took over. It's been three years since the revolution, but it might as well have been yesterday to a woman whose son was killed in the conflict. Then check the mail at the post office next door. The mail is always one of two things: a letter from her sister Evelyn in New Jersey or a "we have no room for you now, but keep waiting and sending paperwork" dispatch from the US State Department.

—m—

Friday, July 29, 1943, didn't start out special, just another trip down the street for the latest "We regret to inform you." Outside, the church bell sweated in the summer heat and rang three. Mrs. Castillo sat, sullen as always, on the sanctuary steps complaining again about how she can't complain about the new Fascist government. "She sure does a lot of complaining for someone who's not allowed to complain."

"Lila, listen to what he does now, this butcher Franco," Mrs. Castillo ranted shaking her newspaper from North to South, "He kills a priest. A padre. A man of G-d—just shoots him like a dog in the street for speaking against him! Ay, what's happened to this place? You used to know who was with you and who was against you. Now they've got Fascists and Communists and Loyalists and Republicans…it's enough to make you dizzy. You say one wrong thing, and you end up going for a walk up to the mountains and never coming back. And they try to tell us this is better than the war in France? *Jope!*"

It seemed these days that everyone cried for change, but Spain had no more blood to give for another cause. Two years and two million had taken a dreadful toll. But for Mrs. Castillo it took just one—her only son.

"Ay, Lila, you should have seen this place before. It was paradise. I remember my Carlitos used to splash in that fountain over there with his little brown dog. And on that corner the Andaluns would dance a flamenco that could wake the dead. Oh, the dancing! We used to dance so much when this was paradise. Oh, how I remember."

"Señora Castillo," Lea wondered aloud, "why don't you leave? Do like me—go to America. What's left for you here?"

But the old woman just sighed and looked away. "No, Lila, this is my home. The only memory I have of my son. Look there—that's his school. And over there is where he used to ride his bicycle. And in this church, we made his holy communion. No. No, I'll stay. I'll wait. I'm an old woman, but I'll hold on long enough to see this assassin Franco swing from his neck. And after that, I'll dance. Then, when I finish dancing, I can die."

It's the Catalan circle of life—work, dance, die.

The summer sun hung heavy, and the heat had gotten so that Lea had forgotten what she'd started. The day's mail still dangled loosely from her fingertips. It was just one letter that day—stamped in blue and looking rather official.

"Probably more government bullshit," she said silently as she slowly traced her fingertips across the envelope's seal and finished her moment with Mrs. Castillo. It always seemed that her immigration visa would slide two points farther with every letter she'd open. Still with rote routine, she slowly ripped the envelope, glanced down, and gasped. Then... she danced.

WAR!

By 1:45 the danish are launched. My eldest nephew, a sturdy boy of four, has started a quarrel with his young cousin, Jacob. Jacob, it seems, had unwisely offered to share a piece of his black and white cookie with my nephew. Unimpressed with his benefactor's gift, my nephew split the cookie in two and hurled the vanilla half across the table in protest. Lest he stand for so grievous an insult, Jacob returned fire, launching the chocolate half of his cookie and the rest of the Arnie and Richie's Deli day-old danish. World War III has begun and for dessert, we'll be switching to strudel.

Through it all, Uncle Erwin remains cool under fire. With pious resolve, he raises his arms high above the challah and chants the ancient Hebrew prayers, but with dwindling danish, he is fast running out of things to bless. He reaches to his grandson, Jacob, and with a heavy, hairy hand on the boy's shoulder, gingerly explains how Moses would never have thrown a four-dollar box of danish at his cousin—even if he did start it. Then, in a voice that rings with phlegm he cries "Ashrei ha'yeladim simcha!"— "Blessed are the children that bring us such joy!"

From her quiet corner, Bubbie just watches and wallows, pained by the thought that her great-grandson could be the instigator of such a shameful conflict. "Oy, how it hurts me to see vhat's happening mit the children today," she tells me. "I see on the news such terrible tings. Mine children, they never did these tings. They loved each other so much. My Maxie, even when the Germans were trying to kill us, he vas so happy and quiet. And my Fanny—she vas just a little maydela—a little girl—when the var broke out, but she tooked care on her brother and sister like she vas their own mother. Oy, and my little Eva..." She shudders when she mentions Eva. She always shudders when she mentions

Eva. *"Oy, from such tragedies I survive that I should lose my little girl—so young—a beautiful bride to be, kinehora—to colitis."*

She catches a falling tear and fixes her shirt. Then with a deep outward breath she works a smile. "Oh, but you never knew my Eva, Russel," she sighs.

I never did know her. By the time I was born, she was already gone. I know only an image from a withered photograph and the name that my cousin now carries—the echoes of a little girl who loved James Dean and caramel-covered popcorn. I guess there's a lot of me that's just stories and tattered pictures.

But I try to share what I know. I take my nephew by the hand and struggle to explain how his great-grandma used to climb giant mountains in the freezing snow. And as I speak to him, he gazes at me with wondrous brown eyes and with an outstretched arm...he wails my leg with a pepper grinder.

Maybe he's still too young to understand. Yeah, I was four once, too.

CHAPTER XXXIV

WAR

··············

May 27, 1944. Lisbon, Portugal. Maybe by accident, maybe by divine fortune, but Lea managed passage aboard the *Serpa Pinto*, a Portuguese cruiser. They called it a passenger liner, but it was more of a human cargo vessel. Over four hundred people crammed onto a ship meant to carry less than half that many. But it was war, and war is great for business if you're in the business of ferrying refugees. So, every desperate soul who could negotiate a ticket had a spot. To be honest, nobody cared much about accommodations—it was enough just to be sailing to freedom.

Restless passengers gabbed and wondered about their families in the United States, the new lives they would make, and the new things they would see. Would they be able to keep kosher in America? Would they see the Statue of Liberty from the port in Philadelphia? A Ukrainian child even thought the streets were really made of gold. Two days passed that way—idle chitchat and uneventful sailing.

Midnight. Day three at sea. Tranquility was shattered. The passengers woke to the sound of gunfire above the bow of the ship. At first, it was tough to figure out what exactly was happening. The hysterical passengers only made the confusion worse by speculating about the noise.

"The Germans are attacking us!"

"No, the Americans are attacking us!"

"No, we're attacking the Germans!"

No one had a clue. But everyone had a theory, some more plausible than others.

The ship stopped, and again came the gunshots—another round of mortar trailed by an unidentifiable voice on a bullhorn. Some went topside to see what the bullhorn was saying. Most stayed below waiting for an explanation from the captain. The gravelly voice took form as they neared the surface—it was definitely male, definitely German. "Maybe it's better to wait downstairs," Lea decided. So she returned below and listened to the rumor mill churn.

By this point the passengers had figured out that a German U-boat had seized the ship and summoned a tender to bring the purser and passenger manifest. They were definitely looking for someone. It was only left to figure whether they would torpedo the ship once they found him. After all, Portugal was a neutral country, and to fire upon a neutral flag was a flat-out declaration of war.

The debate just made everyone more nervous. Some felt the Germans would leave once they had their man. But most had fled enough ruined cities to know that Hitler never flinched at an opportunity to make war. Mothers cried and clutched their children as the captain made his long-awaited announcement.

"This is the captain. As you are probably aware by now, this ship has been detained by the German navy. Some of my crew have been ordered to accompany the Germans. I will remain on board to see to your safety. I need all of you to do exactly as I say, and we'll be off again soon. This is the captain."

It didn't take long for word to spread that the man they were looking for was an Englishman from Canada named Grande-Perez—an ethnically confused man—no doubt suspected by the Germans of some sort of treachery. Really, no one was sure why exactly they wanted him. The Reich rarely gave explanations, and when it wasn't your name being called, you didn't ask. The order had been issued: find him in the next five minutes, or people start dying. That was all anyone needed to know.

The crew tore through the ship in a desperate hunt for their fugitive as the sailors guided the passengers at gunpoint to the galley. Every head was counted. Anyone on the registry but not accounted for would be found and summarily shot. The Germans were brutally efficient that way. In the distance, echoed the cries of the search party. Hardly a moment passed before they found him. German efficiency was no match for Portuguese desperation.

—⁓—

Hours afloat and awash in the galley of the ship—standing at attention while copper pots swayed back and forth above the shiny steel prep station. At exactly 1:15 p.m., a nervous deckhand delivered the news. They had been given thirty minutes to leave. Ten had already passed, and only one lifeboat had been launched. With all eyes anxiously fixed forward, Captain Dos Santos bellowed the order, "Abandon ship!"

The passengers stormed the narrow metal steps pushing over any man, woman, or child who stood in the way. As they neared the surface, they could hear the Germans calling to load torpedoes and prepare to sink her. Some waited on deck for instructions. Most dove into the cold, rough sea.

Click-click-flash. Atop the circling sub, German soldiers photographed the hysterical refugees as bodies plunged into the dark, choppy waters. Click-click-flash. They just kept snapping as the passengers struggled to tread the rough seas. Click-click-flash. In a panic, still more passengers leaped from the boarding ladder directly to the lifeboat. All the while, the flashbulbs continued to flicker. Click-click-flash. Click-click-flash. A shriek echoed from atop a capsized lifeboat. "Oh G-d, my baby! Oh G-d, my baby! Somebody help!" A fourteen-month-old child slipped through her mother's arms as their lifeboat was swamped. Click-click-flash! Click-click-flash! The spectators helplessly watched as the infant's nine-year-old sister begged, "My sister, my sister, please help, please help her, she's drowning!" Click-click-flash. No one lifted a finger. The pictures just kept on snapping.

In the frenzy, drowning passengers scrambled for anything that would float—which, for the most part, was each other. Those that weren't strong or fortunate enough to swim away from the boat were slammed against its hard steel hull by the merciless tide. They spit salty seawater and gasped for air, as they strained to stay afloat and distance themselves from their only safe haven. Some could see their captain taken prisoner on the deck of the submarine. He was flanked at each side by armed sailors. His face was battered. His stripes had been ripped from his lapel. "Get away from the ship! Get away from the ship!" the captain cried. He didn't doubt for a minute that Hitler had the nerve to sink her.

All the while, Lea watched in horror from high atop the deck of the *Serpa Pinto*. She hadn't jumped because she saw that the crew hadn't. "Surely, these men know better than the lunatics diving into the ocean," she figured, "so I'll follow them." She trailed the sailors as they climbed above the gangway to lower the remaining lifeboats. There were eight boats and nearly four hundred passengers, but it was all they had, so they set them loose. "My children are safe in America. What does it matter now if I die? At least I could help these people." She was the only woman—the only passenger—who stayed to drop lifeboats into the water.

—⋙—

Even the keenest among them would never have seen it coming—a sudden SNAP!—and then, in an instant, a swing block set loose like a thousand-pound baseball bat barreling at the cook's head. Before a muscle could twitch, he had vanished—swallowed quickly and quietly by a merciless tide.

There was no time to mourn, no time to think. The *Serpa Pinta* was still on a certain course to the bottom of the sea. So they did what they could to rally a rescue. By now most were in the ocean fighting to stay afloat—struggling to survive. Only Lea and the crew remained aboard watching and working a plan. One by one, with a woman's help, they twisted big, heavy cranks lowering each lifeboat until all eight were set afloat. Once the last boat was loose, they jumped aboard. Apparently those old fish tales about the sailors going down with the ship never made it to Portugal.

Crazed swimmers weary from treading the violent sea, raced to fill what little space remained in the tenders. The young and strong climbed the backs of the old and weak in the mad rush to fill any open seats. Some fell prey to the delusions that haunt desperate souls who get lost at sea.

A Polish woman cried frantically for her long-dead husband. "No, I won't go without him! He'll come for me." They knew it was easier to lie. "Your husband is on another boat. Now climb in, and we'll take you to him." The job was to get as many people aboard—any way they could.

Women and children huddled cold and wet in the shaky lifeboats while others held life preservers watching as the U-boat circled like an indecisive shark. Lea stayed with the sailors. They kept crackers and wine stashed beneath the chain locker. So, once there was nothing left to do, they ate, drank, and waited.

By now the rumor mill was full turn. Would they sink her? Wouldn't they sink her? Everyone wanted desperately to believe the chief mate that they wouldn't—they couldn't—not with the undersecretary of something or another on board. That would be war.

Still more hours adrift. A strange and anxious quiet had settled over the survivors adrift in the moonlight. And though only the sound of wind and waves seemed to drift through the air, the same conversations managed to ring clear as a bell through the racing imaginations of every refugee and crewman there: "Awaiting orders to scuttle her, Commander. Please respond, over."

"Naval command, respond. Shall we sink her?"

Why? We'll never know. Maybe they took pity. Maybe Hitler already had enough problems that day. But at precisely 8:45 the U-boat decided it was time to go. An announcement was made in what could have passed for Portuguese saying, "Go. You are cleared to pass."

"What? What are they saying?" a worried passenger shouted.

"They're saying it's over. Go back to the ship," a random voice answered.

"No, it's a trick! Don't go," other voices wailed in the distance.

A fear still set in their stomachs that the Nazis would sink them once they reboarded. Frightened Jews cried to the bullhorn, "See, they're so stingy, these Germans, they won't waste the torpedoes unless they know we're on the ship." Only when Captain Dos Santos finally stood at the bow of the boat and promised their safety, did the passengers at last return.

For two more days the sub lurked at their stern like a stalking predator. Over every shoulder she was there—watching—waiting—unsure. But, soon, as swiftly as she appeared, she just vanished back into the ocean—silently swallowed into the bubble of her ring-shaped wake. You could still feel her there behind you, an invisible shadow at their heels, but on the surface there was only the stillness of the sea.

—m—

Maybe it was five, maybe it was ten minutes later when a voice cried out from the deck, "Airplane!—over there—an airplane." Was it friend or foe? Who knew? But it was coming straight for them. "The Germans—they sent a plane to bomb us. See, I told you they wouldn't waste the torpedoes," a nervous mother hollered from the gangway.

In the approaching distance you could hear the churning—a twin-prop bomber on a slow and steady descent cruising straight for them. Her engines hummed, her form grew more crisp and clear with each meter that she gained. Then in an instant, the plane swiped sideways straight above the ship, leveled a hair, and let loose her load. And then it rained. Leaflets tumbled from the sky like a ticker tape parade. "Americans! Americans!" the people cheered. They knew it wasn't the Germans because—well, because everyone knew they hardly ever give messages when they're going to drop a bomb on you.

WHO'S COMPLAINING?

It's just past 2:30, and the Russians are singing again. They've lost most of their audience to the whitefish and a one-day sale at Macy's, but still they keep going.

Bubbie and I are on the couch with Uncle Stanley. The dog's got the easy chair. Aunt Pauline and Grandma Anna have retreated to the dining room for dessert. The Dating Game is on and even they don't have the stomach for Chuck Woolery*.

We've dug into another discussion about the not-so-good old days. It's kind of like watching another exercise in comparative misery.

Bubbie:
Oy, I need to sit for a few minutes. I get dizzy sometimes from the tumor in my head.

Stanley:
You've got a tumor, too?

Bubbie:
Ya, mine sister-in-law, Malcha, gave me this tumor.

It used to be that we'd stop and be puzzled by a statement like that, but we're long past that point.

Bubbie:
In Poland, I vas maybe ten years old, vhen my mother gave my sister and me in to Malcha to babysit. Vell, in those days my sister vas a vild girl—my mother used to call her a "Mishuga Americana"—"a crazy American." Vell, your Tanta Evelyn made a joke on Malcha and put

---

* The overly genial host of the show

a paste on the doorknob so it would stick on Malcha's hand. Oy, Malcha got so mad from this joke that she started throwing the pots from the kitchen. She hit mine sister—boom!—mit a frying pan in the chest and me she hit mit a pot on the head. You know, vhen mine sister died from a heart attack a few years ago they said she had an old black spot on the heart. The doctors, they didn't know vhere it came from—this spot. Ach, these geniuses could have saved a lot of aggravation if they vould have asked me. I tell you it vas Malcha's frying pan vhat made this spot that killed your Tanta Evelyn. You see, and now they tell me I got a tumor in the head vhere she hit me mit that pot.

Stanley:

You know, when I was in school, I was such a bad kid, the teacher used to hit me with a ruler. Then after school I would go to the rabbi for Hebrew lessons, and he would hit me with a book. I'd finally get home to my parents, and they'd hit me with a stick for upsetting the rabbi and the teacher.

Me:

Is that true?

Stanley:

No, but it's a funny story.

Uncle Stanley has this way of spinning even the tensest conversation to a breath of levity—which is good, because I'm really not equipped to add to this discussion. Despite all my petty complaints, I still know I've been blessed. That world of hers—that place of empty crockpots and flying frying pans—is light years *from the swing sets and swimming pools of Miami Beach—so far from my little kosher deli beach town.*

It's finally quiet. Even "strong like bull" Russians need to break for decaf and herring once in a while. Bubbie is sitting upright on the sofa. She has that look of an old lady on a park bench, waiting around, though for nothing in particular.

Stanley:
Lea, you need a ride home?

Bubbie:
No thank you, Stanley. I vant to rest a little bit, then I take the bus.

Stanley:
Are you sure, Lea? Really, it's no trouble.

Bubbie:
Oh no, Stanley, you go. I'll manage mit the bus.

Stanley:
Unbelievable, Lea, how you still schlep around town on those buses.

Bubbie:
I schlep. I schlep. Not so much like I used to. But I don't vant to sit around and do nothing. So, I take the bus to the market. I valk to the river to feed the pigeons. I play cards.

Me:
You still got your card games?

Bubbie:
A few of the old players are still around, but I don't tink I vant to play mit these vomen anymore. Oy, they're so stingy! They fight mit each other for

*nothing—over a penny! Last week I vin a nickel
in a game of calooki, and they got so jealous they
don't speak to me. They say I must be cheating
to be so lucky. First, on Tuesday I vin the three
dollar jackpot in the bingo and now this. They say,
"No, it's too much. It must be a scandal! No one
can be that lucky." Now, the whole fifth floor vants
to make an investigation. Have you ever heard of
such a tings? Ach, I got a mind to tell them "Look,
if it bothers you so much—the nickel—I give you a
qvarter to shut up." Oy, such a chutzpah, I tell you.
Do you know vhat means "chutzpah," Russel?*

I listen to her funny gargly accent, and then it hits me—that accent—that ancient language that for hundreds of years has tethered the world's Jews—is dying. My father knows a few words. I, a few less than he—and so on down the chain. Whatever we were—it's all different now.

Bubbie:

*Oy, Russel, it's changing—mine quiet little
building—so many young people now—Spanish,
Chinese—families mit children. The Jewish people
from mine generation—mine friends, mine brother,
mine sister—they're all gone. From our family, me
and Malcha are the last ones—and she's not doing
so good either. She don't see, she don't hear.*

Me:

I thought she goes dancing on the cruise ships?

Bubbie:

*Ya, this she still does. She dances so much, they
give her free cruises. Vould you believe an eighty-
seven-year-old voman carrying on like that? But I*

tink she goes because she's afraid to stop. It's like vhen they told my brother he vas too old to keep his motorcycle—that's vat finally killed him.

I guess Malcha never hit him with anything.

Bubbie:
He died the same year they made him got rid of that motorcycle. So, no matter how sick she gets, Malcha keeps dancing. If they take her in a vheelchair, she vould still dance.

The music is back, but the chorus has gone the way of the whitefish. I'm just waiting to help Mom clear the table, then I'll probably head off to my own life, too.

Stanley:
Lea, are you sure you don't want a ride?

Bubbie:
No, no. I vait for the bus. I don't vant you should go out of the vay.

Bubbie wants to go, but she's too tired to deal with buses and too proud to ask for help.

Me:
Bubbie, I'm heading to the mall in a few minutes. Why don't you come with me? I'll drop you off on the way.

She smiles with a look of quiet surrender.

Bubbie:
Okay, okay. I let my lawyer take me home. My card players are vaiting for me.

As I round up the silver and Chinese china, I stare at those creased faces—study their labored walks from one resting point to the next—and I'm confused by their joy. As much as they try to respect the time-honored Jewish tradition of complaining, I think that deep down, they're happy. Bubbie, Aunt Pauline, Grandma Anna, Aunt Sara—they're all smiling. Even Toby's got a grin from ear to ear. She can't remember what she's happy about, but she never forgets to smile.

Who knows? Maybe it's not so complicated to understand. Sure, they've had it rough, but like they say, "through the years they've danced and sung, loved and laughed, wept and smiled, and left their children a little better than they started—and I guess at the end of the day there's not much more you can ask for than that."

CHAPTER XXXV
HOMECOMING

....

It was all just outside that rusty railcar. Freedom, family, a new life, and still, she was peering through a dusty window looking out at the lot of it. They had been hauled straight from the port to an abandoned railcar that the Feds had converted to a makeshift interrogation center. At the front of the train, an old, gray, black woman typed away at blazing speed as lines of refugees answered countless questions about the obvious.

"Why did you leave your country of origin?"

"To survive."

"Why America?"

"We needed to survive."

"What will you do here?"

"Survive."

Up and down the train, busy-looking bureaucrats bustled through the railcar shuffling papers as "I'll Be Home for Christmas" buzzed on an old RCA tube radio calling their boys home.

The ship had managed to reach Philadelphia three days and thirteen hours ago, but America was still a giant step away. Army, navy, FBI, State Department. How many people could possibly ask the same questions over and over again?

"Are you, or have you ever been, a member of the communist party?"

"They took my husband—the communists."

"That's terrible, ma'am."

"No, that's the one good thing they done for me."

"Do you support the overthrow of the United States government by force or violence?"

"Force." It sounded better than "violence."

—m—

Cleared at last! The girls rushed to hug their mama, grabbing tightly at her waist. They had grown so much in eighteen months. And Maxie—such a *mensch*—he was a little man already. He stood at Fanny's feet, wearing a little sailor's suit that he tugged at uncomfortably. Lea bent to pick him up. He crept back and clutched his sister's hand. Fanny had to pry his little fingers loose to hand him to his mother. "Maman! Maman!" he cried, reaching for his sister. A year and a half is an eternity to a child.

—m—

It must have been about three days later—an unexpected knock at Evelyn's door. Captain Dos Santos and the crew had come to visit Lea with a bouquet of white roses and a bottle of champagne. The card said simply, "For a hero." Her smile lit up Paterson.

A FAREWELL SALUTE

The crowd has dwindled to a few lingering scavengers left picking at the bones of a tattered whitefish. The coffee pots are empty; the blintzes are cold. Crumbs are all that remain of a delicious apple strudel. Leon's piano playing trails off midsong. An early close to an exhausting day.

Bubbie is by herself on the couch now, watching television, waiting for me. She prefers CNN and politics to game shows but didn't want to make a scene—Grandma Anna and Aunt Pauline so enjoy fighting over those crazy quiz programs. On the news is a spot of President Reagan at a War Memorial in Europe. To most, it's just another sound bite from another stop on another presidential tour—for Bubbie it's much more. She's mesmerized as the Gipper speaks.

"We're here to mark that day in history when the Allied peoples joined in battle to reclaim this continent to liberty. For four long years, much of Europe had been under a terrible shadow. Free nations had fallen, Jews cried out in the camps, millions cried out for liberation. Europe was enslaved, and the world prayed for its rescue. Here the Allies stood and fought against tyranny in a giant undertaking unparalleled in human history."

With a tearful eye and a broken smile, she answers her kindred president, "Oy, Brother, you don't know the half of it!"

THE END

And they lived…"Look, I can't complain. I'm comfortable. It's a little hot here, and maybe you could call a little more often, and isn't it about time you got married. But don't worry about me. I'm okay. I'll manage"…ever after.

FAMILY ALBUM AND PHOTO EPILOGUE

Me and Bubbie (the expression says it all)

Bubbie arrives in America to her kids

Isaac with Esther and the dog

Fanny's visit to Camp Des Milles.   The family on the run in France.

Avram and Jacob toasting victory.
After the war Jacob tried living here in America a
few times. But each time he'd return to Belgium.
"You've got to kill yourself working here," he'd tell Bubbie.
He died from a heart attack soon after at the age of 50.
He was having a drink with his brother at the time.

Uncle Abe on his motorcycle.
Note the homemade helmet and garbage-can windshield. Uncle Abe lived a long happy life doing something
"useful" – he worked as a barber on Miami Beach.

Bubbie and Dad. Dad started out as a barber with Uncle
Abe and later decided to switch to another "useful" trade.
He became a building contractor and all-around fix it guy.

Eva before she passed at age 21

The girls in Belgium

Bubbie and husband #3

Evelyn, Bubbie and Sam

Jacob and Avram (1947)

Lazega family exhibit at a war museum in Aix-en-Provence, France

Old friends: Bubbie and Rosie.
Rosie lived to the ripe old age of fifteen.
She died fat, smart, and happy.

Leon at his piano. Still playing music at eighty-something years old. Both of Abe's children followed in the family tradition – cutting hair.

Bubbie "dancing on my wedding" with her granddaughter, Evie (Fanny's daughter). Of course, as always, for special occasions– a red dress.

Fanny (now "Faye") and Erwin – happy as always. Faye and Erwin started a successful art gallery on Miami Beach and helped revive Miami Beach's famed Lincoln Road art district.

Grandma Anna.
Grandma Anna lived to age seventy-seven, when her heart finally gave out. To the end, she sold books she never read and cherished long fights with the sister she wasn't "talkin' to".

Grandma Anna with Aunt Pauline. Aunt Pauline stayed ornery, raunchy
and full of laughs until Alzheimer's took her in the year 2000.

Sara and Toby in deep discussion– at times with each other. Sara lived with
her wit sharp and her heart kind until the age of ninety-five. Toby lost more
and more of her memory as time passed but she never stopped entertaining
us with her songs– even when she forgot the words, and sometimes even
when she forgot the music. Uncle Stanley's eulogy for her, titled *How do you
eulogize your mother?* was his most touching ever.

Uncle Stanley. All smiles. We lost him too soon to cancer in 2008. But I guess we were all blessed that a man who had been told at age twenty-nine that the tumors in his lungs would take him before age thirty, somehow managed to stick around and make us laugh for another forty-seven years.

The Lazega Family: My sister Betsy (sans green hair) (psychologist in Florida), Me (lawyer in Florida), Mom (working with me in Florida), Bubbie (passed away in 2006), Dad (retired contractor in Florida), and my brothers Jay (lawyer in Atlanta) & Hymie (still in need of a psychologist).

My Family: Russ, Kassie, Leslie
(without her crucifix), Ethan

Me in my favorite place

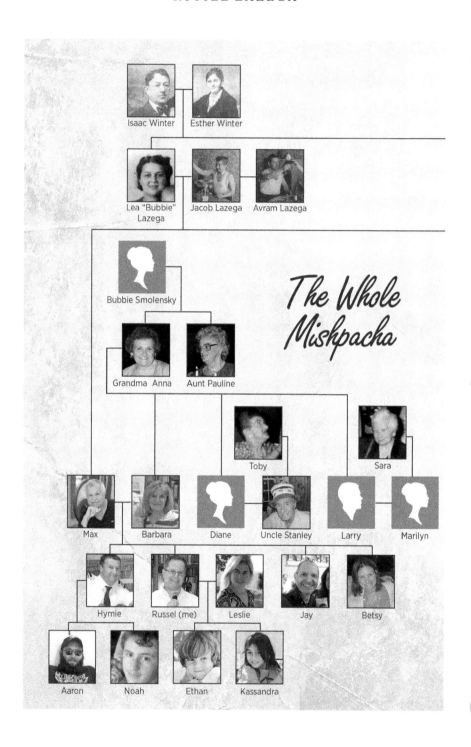

Uncle Abe   Malcha   Evelyn   Ronald Reagan???

Fannie   Uncle Erwin   Eva   Leon   Mira

Cousin Ron   Cousin Linda   Cousin Evie   Cousin Lyle

Cousin Ari
"Arielle"

Jacob

FAMILY TREE OF
Lea Winter Lazega

Our family tree is actually larger but to avoid confusion, this
abreviated version contains just those characters mentioned in the book
(or family that need to be mentioned in order to show how characters are related).

AUTHOR'S NOTE

···

At times I wish I'd billed this book as fiction. The fact is that the details of this book are probably 98% accurate but invariably, I will no doubt hear from the critics about the 2% where memories of names, places, colors, and sounds are inaccurate or incomplete, or historical accounts diverge depending on who is telling the story. So let me set the record straight here: This book is a collage of Bubbie's memories and the memories of the people who surrounded her. While I dedicated over a decade to researching and making this book as accurate as possible, it is still based on first, second and sometimes third-hand accounts of ancient people and ancient memories. And like any memory there are sure to be gaps and conflicts. There are also times where it was necessary to reconstruct and fill in the gaps. Sometimes names, places and dates are a best guess meant to keep the heart of the story true. At times, some characters' names were changed to protect an identity. And in some cases, I had only a first name (or no name at all) to work with.

So remember, if you and your lawyer are thumbing through this book and thinking, "hey, that's me" or "that's my great-uncle Moe." Know that it's probably not. So, just sit back and enjoy the read. You can call it fiction if it makes you feel better.

ACKNOWLEDGEMENTS

This endeavor has been a decade-long labor of love for me. It has taken time from personal and professional life to weave together and bring to fruition and I am exceedingly grateful to my family in this book (whose salt and pepper perspectives have brought color to my life and these pages), to my family at home (my wife, Leslie, my two children, Kassie and Ethan, and my three dogs (who occasionally bite me but otherwise have been a great source of comfort and support), to my spectacular editor Victoria from Create Space for just helping make this book better, to David Sinai and his team at Picsera for breathing life into old forgotten photos, and finally to the friends like June Azoulay, George Kalinsky, J.D. Underwood, Michael Tuccitto, Robin Willner, Harvey Schneider, Elaine Adler, Sue Kovach, Kristine Flurry, Arnie Preston, Lisa Beer, Dr. Robin Roth and Senator Steve Geller who all read this book and then read it again —never faltering in their belief that this is a story to be shared.

Author Russel Lazega is a lawyer living in North Miami Beach, Florida. He is a columnist for the *Aventura* News and the author of several nonfiction publications, including *Florida Motor Vehicle No-Fault Law and Practice (PIP)*, the nation's leading treatise on Florida car insurance law that stirred tremendous excitement throughout Florida's bustling community of insurance agents and insurance lawyers. *Managing Bubbie* is Lazega's first foray into creative nonfiction. When he is not writing, or chasing after a pair of fire-breathing, house-wrecking T. rexes that claim to be small children, the author can be found kayaking the waterways of South Florida, venturing as far as the tide will take him from his loving, but indescribably overbearing, family.

CPSIA information can be obtained
at www.ICGtesting.com
Printed in the USA
BVHW041827010319
541087BV00013B/94/P